PRIVATE SOLDIERS
AND PUBLIC HEROES

AN AMERICAN ALBUM OF THE COMMON MAN'S CIVIL WAR

FROM THE PAGES OF CIVIL WAR TIMES ILLUSTRATED

Edited by Milton Bagby

Foreword by John E. Stanchak • Introduction by Harold Holzer

Published in Nashville, Tennessee, by Rutledge Hill Press, 211 Seventh Avenue North, Nashville, Tennessee 37219. Distributed in Canada by H. B. Fenn & Company, Ltd., 34 Nixon Road, Bolton, Ontario L7E 1W2. Distributed in Australia by The Five Mile Press Pty., Ltd., 22 Summit Road, Noble Park, Victoria 3174. Distributed in New Zealand by Tandem Press, 2 Rugby Road, Birkenhead, Auckland 10. Distributed in the United Kingdom by Verulam Press, Ltd., 152a Park Street Lane, Park Street, St. Albans, Hertfordshire AL2 2AU.

Design and typography by Jeff King, Harrisburg, Pennsylvania.

Library of Congress Cataloging-in-Publication Data

Private soldiers and public heroes : an American album of the common man's Civil War / edited by Milton Bagby.
    p. cm.
  ISBN 1-55853-688-4 (hc)
    1. United States—Armed Forces—History—Civil War, 1861–1865—Pictorial works. 2. Confederate States of America—Armed Forces—History—Pictorial works. 3. Soldiers—United States—History—19th century—Pictorial works. 4. Soldiers—Confederate States of America—Pictorial works. 5. United States—History—Civil War, 1861–1865—Personal narratives. I. Milton, Bagby, 1947– .
E607.P75 1998
973.7'42—dc21   98-27465
                                                CIP

Printed in Hong Kong through Palace Press.

1 2 3 4 5 6 7 8 9—02 01 00 99 98

Dedicated to the common men and common soldiers of the American Civil War.

CONTENTS

FOREWORD

I F YOU WERE A NATIVE-BORN AMERICAN, in 1861 you saw it coming. In this country each generation had had its war. It was something like a regularly scheduled test...of commitment, of manhood, of loyalty. Up until then, the enemies had been the French, the Indians, the British, and the Mexicans. The objectives had been to protect land, free land, or grab land. But the test questions were always the same: Were you game for the fight, and were you loyal...to your neighbors, your town, your people?

In December 1860 the state of South Carolina seceded from the Union. By Christmas, this public decision brought on an armed crisis in the state's largest city, Charleston. U.S. Army troops stationed there withdrew to Fort Sumter, a large brick fortress set on an island of rubble in the middle of Charleston Harbor. The fort's commander, Maj. Robert Anderson, refused to surrender it to the Secessionists, who claimed it and all other U.S. property in the state belonged to the people of South Carolina.

As the days and weeks passed other Southern states seceded, allied themselves with South Carolina, and laid the groundwork for the establishment of a new, separate nation, the Confederate States of America. Meanwhile, cannon ringing Charleston Harbor were loaded up by South Carolinians and trained on Fort Sumter and its small garrison. Events quickly reached an impasse. Newly elected president of the United States Abraham Lincoln said the acts of South Carolina were outside the law. South Carolina Secessionists claimed they were within their rights and wanted all their property. Anderson said he would not give up the fort; he and his men would stand by their constitutional duty.

America was ready for its next war. This time, though, the objective had little to do with protecting, freeing, or grabbing land. It had to do with the supremacy of an idea: Was America destined to be one country or two? And this time, the threat to the peace came from other Americans. Depending on where you made your home, the rascals who needed a sound beating lived in either the North or the South of the old United States itself, not in France, Britain, or south of the Rio Grande. The test endured by each generation, however, went unchanged and its questions were still put to every free man in America: Were you game for the fight and were you loyal?

The reflexive answer was a loud yes! But ready to fight whom, and loyal to what?

On April 12, 1861, Secessionist troops around Charleston Harbor opened fire on Fort Sumter. What followed we know today as the Civil War. The names of the men who wrote its policies and engineered its battlefield victories are still taught to American schoolchildren: Lincoln, Davis, Sherman, Jackson, Grant, and Lee. But the names and the faces of the three million men who fought it and the millions at home who supported and nurtured them are almost forgotten. *Civil War Times Illustrated*, a magazine for fans of Civil War history, is one of the few publications where they are regularly honored and their service recalled. For more than fifteen years it has published a popular column, once called "Time Lapse" and now named "Gallery," in which the faces of common people who took part in the conflict are displayed in antique photographs and their humble, sometimes sad, sometimes inspiring, sometimes heroic personal stories are set down in a few words. There they get to be remembered one last time.

The common man's America in 1861. That year it claimed two capital cities. For those loyal to the old Union, there was Washington, D.C., with its uncompleted Washington Monument {above} and unfinished Capitol dome {right}. March 4 that year, Abraham Lincoln of Illinois, a well-to-do corporate lawyer who came from a "common" background, was sworn in as president of the United States. In this photograph, taken at about 1:30 on a cloudy afternoon, he stands at the podium taking the oath of office from Chief Justice Roger B. Taney, a cash-poor Maryland aristocrat who disliked common man Lincoln's views.

This book is a collection of those photographs and stories and is dedicated to their memory. The images of these common people and the details of their experiences are supplied by descendants or by collectors of photographs and memorabilia who have done supportive research. The work is divided into chapters that help define who these people were and what their stories are about. They are titled "Volunteers," "Common Soldiers," "Uncommon Men," "Sacrifices," and "Veterans." When you reach the last word, you will understand that these men never unanimously agreed on who their enemy was or what threatened them. But you will know their reasons for taking up the fight were simple and clear. For most it was all about a sense of obligation and a sense of place. They were loyal to their homes and neighbors.

How else can you explain a fellow like Henry Brown, someone readers meet in "Uncommon Men"? A free black South Carolinian, he marched off with his town's all-white company and willingly and proudly served as its drummer until the war's end. He ignored every opportunity to escape to a calm place behind Union lines, set aside the race questions of the day, and later took a civil post during Reconstruction, looking out for the needs of his defeated white neighbors. How else can you understand what motivated Joseph Pierce, another of the "Uncommon Men." A Chinese boy brought to Connecticut by a sea captain, adopted and raised as a New Englander, Pierce was perhaps the only Asian-American man to serve in the Union's Army of the Potomac. He marched off to the war with his Connecticut townsmen not to prove anything in particular, but simply because he knew he was one of them and believed he should share their burden.

You will meet no nationally prominent men or women here, but you might come to appreciate a bitter remark, common on the streets and in the fields in those days in both the North and South, that called the great conflict "a rich man's war and a poor man's fight." Usually, the people remembered in this book are the "poor" who did the fighting and made most of the sacrifices.

In those days, when Northerners with enough cash could hire substitutes to take their place in the army and Southern men owning more than twenty slaves were exempted from the draft, that the humble should do most of the risk-taking just seemed part of the natural order of things. Take William Day, for instance, someone readers come across in "Common Soldiers." An illiterate farmer, not a man of means, he joined the 54th North Carolina Infantry and served long after other men in his unit deserted. Stubborn to his duty, he had his photograph taken in uniform and dictated letters home to his wife and four children explaining why he could not be with them. He fought through the battles of Fredericksburg and Chancellorsville then died unglamorously in Virginia of typhoid — lost to the natural order of things. Or consider Stephen Caitlin, recalled in "Sacrifices." A middle-aged carpenter from Illinois, he joined the Union army after his two sons enlisted, leaving his wife and daughters at home to get along as best they could. His oldest boy died in the mighty 1862 Battle of Shiloh. In the fall of 1863, Stephen Caitlin was gunned down in a skirmish in Farmington, Tennessee. When reenlistment time came, the remaining Caitlin boy didn't sign up again; the Caitlins seemed to be running out of luck and at least one man was needed at home. This, too, was part of the natural order of things. A family had an obligation to survive.

Brown, Pierce, Day, Caitlin, and the other men readers will find here were all tested. Not all of them passed, not many of them were rewarded, very few were covered in glory, but their pictures and their stories represent the millions of others who will never be seen or heard. By appearing here they stand by one last duty, a duty to history. They speak for the experience of Civil War America's common man. ✪

*For the common man loyal to the South and to his neighbors below the Mason-Dixon Line, there was Montgomery, Alabama, the first seat of the new Confederate government. The Alabama state capitol {**opposite**} stood in as a Confederate national symbol on February 18, 1861, when Jefferson Davis of Mississippi stood on its portico in front of a cheering crowd and took the oath of office as provisional president of the Confederate States of America while bands played "Dixie." This photograph of the event is believed to be the only one to survive into our time. For reasons still baffling to many analysts and historians, on May 20 the Confederate Congress voted to move the capital from the relative safety of Montgomery in central Alabama to Richmond, Virginia, a city just one hundred miles from Washington, D.C.'s hostile armies.*

In the common man's America of 1861, the armies were made up of civilian volunteers, not military professionals.
Both Confederate and Union forces were built on old state militia organizations, outfits superb at parades and picnics, not at military campaigns.

....

Right: *For example, an unidentified militia unit photographed at New York City's 1860 Independence Day parade*
dressed lavishly and appeared to march well but probably had never seen combat.

....

Above: *The Kentucky State Militia was photographed at its August 1860 encampment.*
The refreshment stand in the upper left corner of this photo hints its troops had a soft approach to military affairs.

In the 1860s the common man's America offered everything from urban to rustic conditions. Photographs of New York City {left} and Los Angeles {above} produced in those years made this fact clear. The amateur soldiers profiled here hailed from these places and others. Typical of the Civil War's military men, they claimed both city and country roots.

City or country, in the 1860s the common man's America was a place of hard work:
{clockwise, from left} lumbering, metalwork, railroading, planting, and more.
The men who fought the Civil War practiced professions ranging from the law and
farming to the clergy. Many of their stories explain that their war experiences changed
their approach to making a living. Writing after the conflict, some vowed never to
leave their farms or shops again while others—changed by the years of risk-taking —
became entrepreneurs or swore they would only pursue work they loved.

The faces of America's common men during the Civil War.

*Young Arkansas Confederates {**opposite**}, obviously friends and neighbors, pose for a studio photograph before setting out on campaign.*

*Disheveled refugees from eastern Tennessee {**above, left**}, men who stood by the Union at great personal loss, have the camera document their condition and their personal bond.*

*The working people of Pittsburgh, Pennsylvania {**above, right**}, gather in front of a Fifth Avenue newspaper office to wait for news from the battle front.*

INTRODUCTION

JUST SIX MONTHS BEFORE THE START of the Civil War, a former photographic plate polisher named James Wallace Black took an exhilarating flight in aeronaut Samuel King's hot-air balloon, *Queen of the Air*. Aloft, he carefully aimed his primitive camera at the vast cityscape of Boston below. Then and there, on October 13, 1860, Black made the very first aerial photograph in the United States.

New England writer and philosopher Ralph Waldo Emerson was mesmerized by the picture. "Boston, as the eagle and the wild goose see it, is a very different object from the same place as the solid citizen looks up at its eaves and chimneys," he marveled. "Windows, chimneys, and skylights attract the eye...exquisitely defined, bewildering in numbers." Emerson, the city's resident sage, pronounced the maiden attempt at photography-from-the-skies "a remarkable success," but he could not resist adding he hoped better and more frequent results would someday be "accomplished in the same direction."

That day arrived with breathtaking speed. Emerson was probably astonished that within two years photographers were routinely riding the skies taking bird's-eye pictures for military purposes. In 1862 as North battled South on the Virginia Peninsula below Richmond, Union camera operators hanging from spy balloons made aerial reconnaissance photographs of Confederate troops massing to defend the Southern capital. It was a milestone in military science and in the history of the camera art.

The Civil War, aptly called the first modern war, revolutionized American photography. Its impact on this new medium proved subtle as well as grand. It showed in small details as well as panoramas. It manifested itself in character interpretation as well as in technique and technical innovation. It transformed photographers from technicians into pioneers almost overnight. Cameramen North and South instantly embraced a new spirit in image-making, and that spirit was definitely democratic.

The war's first shots were fired in April 1861. Up to that time, photography had remained a rigid, formal craft practiced almost exclusively in studios for an upscale clientele. For more than a generation, prosperous families had donned their finest clothes and visited prestigious galleries of artists such as Southworth and Hawes in Boston to sit for a formal portrait. Those earliest photographic processes, however, yielded just a single, jewel-like finished image from each lengthy exposure. The photographs were not circulated. They were displayed in the home with the same regard families usually reserved for a formal oil painting.

In those days, busy American cities such as Philadelphia or Charleston boasted growing populations of professional photographers. Future innovators like James Wallace Black were apprenticed to photographic entrepreneurs like Boston's John Adams Whipple, men who remained firmly in the thrall of the rich and famous, the people who could afford their work. The wealthy, however, lost their grip on the soul of the art in 1861. In that year, just as secession began dividing Americans, photography ironically devised a means to bring them closer together. The means arrived in the form of a new photographic craze from France, the revolutionary carte de visite. The carte was a small, visiting card size paper print pasted to a cardboard mount, a print that could be endlessly reproduced from a single negative. The person who paid for the photographic sitting could keep the original print and trade extras with family and friends. Photographs were no longer as rare and precious as ivory miniatures. The carte liberated the medium.

Suddenly, America went wild for photographs and its people rushed to galleries to have their pictures made. Publishers quickly introduced leather books to preserve and display the new images, launching the fashion for family photo albums, items still popular today. Photo studios also mass produced camera studies of military, political, and theatrical celebrities, images they retailed

---

Opposite: *Black's famous aerial photograph of pre–Civil War Boston.*
The "collodion wet plate" process that he and the best-known wartime photographers used allowed him to make an exposure in five to thirty seconds. This process competed with and eventually replaced the previously popular daguerreotype method, the process that required a longer exposure and created only one precious, irreplaceable image.

through newsstands. These shots were meant to occupy honored places in home albums alongside portraits of sweethearts, parents, and children.

It is a tribute to the nation's entrepreneurial spirit that when American men marched off to battle that year, many photo businesses marched off with them. Until the war ended in spring 1865, cameramen traveled with the armies, operating out of both military headquarters and occupied cities, from tents, shacks, and canvas-covered wagons. The country's best remembered Civil War–era photographer, Mathew Brady, called his own cumbersome studio on wheels the "What Is It?" wagon.

Keeping up with marching armies was no small accomplishment, nor was the ability to see beyond the big battles and the great heroes of the day. Photographers, however, did see beyond to the nameless thousands who did the actual fighting. They were a marketing bonanza. The work of the camera operators gave the men in blue and gray the opportunity to immortalize themselves on campaign—and to send the results back to their loved ones at home. To serve the market photographers learned to expose stereographic views (an early foray in 3-D), large-format paper prints, the cartes de visite and—for the soldiers who demanded

Opposite: *A prewar panorama of prosperous Charleston, South Carolina, the city that nursed the secession movement to life. At the time of the Fort Sumter crisis, it supported several professional photographers. In February 1861, just weeks before the shooting started, one of them — George S. Cook — rowed out to the fort and convinced its commander and officers to pose for him. He later joked that fort commander Maj. Robert Anderson surrendered to his camera long before he gave up to the Confederate army.*

....

Above, left: *Downtown Philadelphia's banking district just before the Civil War. From the late 1840s photographers documented life in this American city and here made some of the earliest photos of news events. Mid-nineteenth-century newspapers could not, however, reproduce camera work. Instead, photographers displayed newsworthy photographs in their shop windows to attract business.*

....

Above, right: *Richmond, Virginia, in the mid-1800s, St. Paul's Episcopal Church in the background. This historic intersection attracted nineteenth-century photographers because it was a popular gathering place through the Civil War years and because St. Paul's played a part in events. In April 1865, Confederate President Jefferson Davis was there when a messenger interrupted the services to tell him Union troops were marching on Richmond. That moment signaled the end of Confederate government in the city.*

something indestructible to carry with them in knapsacks and to mail to admirers they left behind—that sturdy standby, the tintype. Whatever the specific photograpic process, common soldiers emerged as the principal subjects of the cameraman's art. The reason was simple: They were the most dependable subjects. They stood still, out of harm's way, and paid cash.

Civil War photographers, even the most celebrated among them (Brady, Alexander Gardner, George N. Barnard, and Timothy O'Sullivan to name four) never quite summoned the technology or daring to observe the war close-up. Wisely, they avoided shot and shell. It was simply too dangerous to set up a tripod and hide beneath a light-resistant cloth in the way of rifle and cannon fire so intense it routinely killed hundreds at a time, gunfire sometimes so concentrated it had been known to level groves of trees. Besides, their plates required so long to expose that pictures of moving armies would have reproduced as mere blurs.

Instead, camera operators concentrated their attention on war at the margins: the portrait of the proud recruit holding his rifle, the drummer boy cradling his treasured instrument, the new volunteer dressed in his splendid dress uniform, comrades in arms posing in camp. Then there were the hideous pictures of the battle dead littering the field after their armies had withdrawn, anonymous, swollen cadavers offering a nightmarish reality check for citizens living far from the front lines. These pictures changed the way people recorded and remembered the terrible experience of war.

Influenced by both gruesome documentary photos and spirit-lifting camp portraits, Americans on both the Northern and Southern home fronts began seeing and acknowledging the sacrifices and dedication of the common soldier. The devotion of these men came to symbolize this new kind of war, just as the old-fashioned concept of gallantry by commissioned officers had dominated romanticized conflicts of the past. Civil War photographers helped make soiled, rumpled, even tattered uniforms seem as gloriously, inspiringly military as gleaming brass, dress swords, and epaulets. The new hero had a daring but appropriate new image for a new era — unglamorous, gritty, and altogether persuasive.

People today are sometimes reminded of something that bears repeating here: The famous photographs of the battlefield dead were always taken in relative safety the day after the fighting stopped. Cameramen were also known to move and even stack bodies to make their compositions more graphic. They manipulated living subjects: Some views of soldiers who appear to be standing outdoors were actually posed in front of makeshift studio backdrops, painted sets that simulated the campsites outside, but without the flies, horses, and other mobile distractions. While this routine manipulation of reality usually hasn't posed many problems for historians, there have been some notable exceptions. For instance, there is a Gardner photograph that was once commonly believed to be the first picture of a battle in progress. After research, this shot turned out instead to show artillery reserves maneuvering their guns the morning after the Battle of Antietam. What had been believed to be cannon smoke in the foreground proved to be nothing more than early morning fog.

To Civil War–era photo buyers, such details hardly seemed to matter: Never before had the commitment of ordinary soldiers to their cause been so widely recorded

A carte de visite, the new format that made photos affordable and popular in America.

Opposite, top: *A photographic entrepreneur in winter quarters with the Union army: a view of a "photographic gallery" run by a G. G. Walker on the edge of the Great Dismal Swamp near Suffolk, Virginia, in December 1863.* Opposite, bottom: *One of Mathew Brady's "What Is It?" wagons, parked in the shade near Manassas, Virginia, on July 4, 1862. The fellow standing beside it taking a drink is Timothy O'Sullivan, a great independent photographer in his own right, who at that point worked as a camera operator for Brady. O'Sullivan received no printed credit on his work. He split with Brady over this artistic integrity issue.*

in a visual medium. The subjects were genuine, even if the circumstances behind many of the sittings were not. As historian James M. McPherson has convincingly demonstrated, the typical common soldier believed in his cause and comrades as passionately as did the generals and politicians. One Ohio volunteer explained his willingness to risk death in battle: "My country had a demand on me." Photographers sensed the passion and patriotism that inspired these soldiers long before historians did.

It is true that Brady never got close enough to a battle to record it with a camera (though, ever the promoter, he later claimed otherwise). Nonetheless, his operators and their competitors managed brilliantly to vivify the war, in part by immortalizing its fighting men. They proved to be the most genuine subjects in the visual annals of the conflict. One reviewer, passing judgment on Brady's early war pictures, wrote that for any "photographer who follows in the wake of modern armies, whatever he represents must be real," even if it was confined to "conditions of repose," not action. The reviewer also wisely understood, "The private soldier has just as good a likeness as the general." Civil War photography had made "the private soldier" a public hero at last.

It was not unusual for a war photographer to specialize in souvenir portraits of companies and regiments in the field. G. H. Houghton of Brattleboro, Vermont, for example, began traveling with a home state regiment during the 1862 Peninsula campaign. He made a series of pictures of the men in camp and in formation, then took the results home to New England to sell to their relatives and friends. As Houghton knew, no other medium made what these men were doing so immediate and so real. No other medium could more dramatically capture the fratricidal nature of the conflict. Another camp photographer, James F. Gibson, was on the scene one day when a Confederate prisoner recognized one of his Union captors and sat down next to him to talk about the old days. Gibson

quickly took their picture, inspiring the captured Rebel to call out: "The picture ought to be called, 'Both Sides, The Cause.'" So it was when it was engraved and nationally distributed by the pictorial newspaper *Harper's Weekly*.

Celebrating the common soldier was a novel notion before the Civil War got under way. As another nineteenth-century critic explained, Americans had been so long accustomed to "reading histories written purely from a general's point of view" that the "idea of the individuality of the soldier is very new to the modern mind." Photographers helped introduce that notion and cement it in the public consciousness through the visual arts. Survivors and descendants preserved the results and passed on the precious archives to succeeding generations.

Now, on the following pages, they may be seen again, resurrected from the past, often by families who have privately treasured them ever since the guns were stilled. They are assembled here in a collection that constitutes an American family album of unsung Civil War heroes. Here are Northerners and Southerners, men and women, whites and blacks, volunteers as well as draftees, proud veterans and maimed survivors.

Largely ignored by history and forgotten by time, they were remembered by photography. The camera not only recorded them. It ennobled them. ✪

Left: *The standard soldier portrait: a determined look and a pose with a weapon. Shots like this one of Pvt. E. E. House of the 38th North Carolina Infantry, a Peninsula campaign veteran, were the bread-and-butter work of Civil War–era field photographers.*
Right: *The long-misinterpreted photograph by Alexander Gardner, a shot that viewers once wrongly believed showed artillery in action at the September 17, 1862, Battle of Antietam near Sharpsburg, Maryland.*

One of Gettysburg's dead, memorialized by then-independent cameraman Timothy O'Sullivan on July 5, 1863.
The battle ended the afternoon of July 3. Civil War photo history authority William C. Davis wrote that the picture "shows a Georgia
Confederate disemboweled and dismembered by a Federal shell. O'Sullivan probably placed the shell and rifle in the picture."

Two pieces of work by enterprising New England photographer G. H. Houghton, showing men of the 4th Vermont Infantry.

Above: *In Virginia, they strike casual camp poses.*
Right: *In the field men of the 4th's Company A show the camera, and the folks at home, how they meet a charge with fixed bayonets.*

"Both Sides, The Cause"

A photograph famous in its day for symbolizing how the war split apart friendships and the nation. The captured Confederate officer is Lieutenant J. B. Washington. His prewar friend and former West Point classmate seated to his left is Union Capt. George Custer, then unknown to American newspaper readers. Lieutenant Washington was captured May 31, 1862, at the Battle of Fair Oaks, Virginia, also known as the Battle of Seven Pines.

CHAPTER I
VOLUNTEERS

CHAPTER I
VOLUNTEERS

THEY ARE HONORED with statues and monuments in every state from Texas to Maine. They are eulogized on all the high patriotic holidays. They are remembered in speeches delivered by school children and by presidents. They are the volunteers who filled the ranks of America's Civil War armies. Yet in the more than 135 years that have passed since civil war broke out in America, the image of who these people were has started to slip from the national memory.

Today, most take it on faith that they were tough, outdoor types; wholesome, unsophisticated individuals loyal to their God and to an idea of what the North or South represented.

Sometimes this is an accurate portrait of the common man in the Civil War and sometimes it is not. The Northern and Southern armies also had their share of city boys, opportunists, family men, literary types, the unschooled, craftsmen, entrepreneurs, fellows who jumped on this opportunity to get away from their families, individuals with political or religious missions, and those just determined not to miss out on what they believed would be the adventure of their lives. Along with diaries, letters, personal stories, and photographs like those shown here, statistics are all we have today to enhance our understanding of who those volunteers were.

Three million men. That's the rough estimate historians make for the number who bore arms during the Civil War. That figure breaks down to about three Union soldiers to every Confederate. It includes a few thousand professional soldiers and sailors, some foreign adventurers, thousands of recent immigrants, and more than a few unusually ambitious guys who hoped a stint in the army would help them get a hold on a better life. Far more than two million of those soldiers were what used to be called "just folks," regular guys, common men.

Both the North and the South instituted a military draft—the Confederacy going first in the spring of 1862, followed by the Union in the summer of 1863. But the largest number of men serving in both the Union and Confederate armed forces were volunteers. They came from every walk of society, a society that the 1860 census claimed was made up of more than thirty-one million people, black and white, free and slave.

The late historian E. B. Long compiled and digested statistics on America's Civil War volunteers and published them in his landmark work *The Civil War Day by Day: An Almanac*. There he recorded that better than 98 percent of the enlisted men were between the ages of eighteen and forty-six and represented the demographic makeup of America at the time. Most were native born. Of the Northerners, about a quarter listed their occupation as "mechanic"—in that day meaning artisans and anyone who worked with machinery—and almost half called themselves farmers. The remainder were laborers (16 percent), business and sales people (5 percent), professionals (3 percent), and those who defied being lumped into a broad category (4 percent).

Records for Dixie's volunteers are incomplete. Many Southern state and county records were destroyed in the closing days of the war, but some Confederate national records did survive. Researchers poring over those papers and local courthouse records concluded more Southerners were involved in agriculture. A lot of the differences ended there. Whether Secessionists cared to admit it or not, the South and North were tied together by some very strong cultural rope.

The volunteers hailed from a continent largely inhabited by folks with strong Anglo-Saxon roots, people who believed in a stern Protestant deity and stood by a Puritan work ethic. In 1860 this latter concept, that a man should be raised up by his own labor and not necessarily by the labor of others, accounted for one broad American sentiment. It was rare to meet someone comfortable with the idea of slavery. Nationally, less than 12 percent had any involvement with individuals or businesses connected to slavery, and according to census

Fort Sumter, photographed by F. K. Houston of Charleston, the day after its formal surrender to South Carolina troops.
This same day President Abraham Lincoln issued a call to the states to provide seventy-five thousand militia volunteers to put down the rebellion.

figures and later studies, in the South 75 percent of the white population had no interest in or connection to slavery. According to Long's study, just ten thousand American families made up the bulk of the nation's slaveholders. They were, however, an influential lot. More than 38 percent of all Southerners were held in slavery, and in the states of Mississippi and South Carolina whites were outnumbered by the slave population.

Modern Americans are quick to say slavery was repugnant. But today it is sometimes forgotten that this was not the issue that kicked off the Civil War. The deadly argument started over the secession of South Carolina and its claim, and later the claim of ten other states, that it was not bound to abide by the U.S. Constitution. South Carolina's determination to make its point by seizing Fort Sumter in Charleston Harbor, a

U.S. Army facility, was the event that sparked the four-year conflict and provoked three million men to make their mark on history.

The fort fell to the South Carolinians in April 1861. By then Southern leaders had already called for one hundred thousand army volunteers. With Fort Sumter in Secessionist hands, U.S. President Abraham Lincoln asked loyal Union men to sign up for military service. The farmers, mechanics, and others who answered these calls had no idea what was in store for them. High on the excitement of the moment, they put on homemade military uniforms, organized themselves into companies, elected their own officers, and marched off to settle the issue. Photography, a fairly new technology, preserved their looks of pride and enthusiasm as they set off on the great crusade of their century. ✪

Recruiting out west. The dragnet for volunteers was cast out across the continent. The war would go everywhere, even to sparsely settled New Mexico Territory, where there were seventy-five engagements. It has long been believed these unidentified men are Confederate army recruits.

A Mississippi recruit. All classes joined up in early 1861 when military amateurs figured this war would resemble a cross between a big picnic and a hunting trip. Like this fellow, the well-to-do came to war in fancy hats and tailor-made uniforms.

May 1, 1861: Detroit gives the 1st Michigan a big send-off as flags are presented to the regiment.
Early in the war, in villages as well as cities, hundreds of volunteer regiments, North and South, enjoyed similar ceremonies.

Ready to fight, Selma's Independent Blues pose in their finery a month after Alabama seceded and two months before the first shots would be fired at Fort Sumter.

Above: *A determined Rebel cavalryman displays typical early-war arms:*
revolvers, a shotgun, and a gut-tearing D-guard Bowie knife
made by a hometown blacksmith.

Opposite: *A Secessionist outfit drawn up for service during the Fort Sumter*
crisis: the Charleston Zouave Cadets in Castle Pinckney,
a Cooper River fort with its cannon aimed at Fort Sumter's back door.

Families got caught up in war fever, and everyone wanted to look the part of a volunteer. Confederate Colonel Archer Anderson's son John sports a child's uniform and saber.

*Young women of the Pennsylvania
Academy of Fine Arts volunteer
their own unique services,
sending the boys off to war
with an outsized handsewn flag.*

THOMAS C. SHEPPARD

....

Eighteen-year-old Thomas C. Sheppard wore his new uniform for this picture shortly after he enlisted in the Confederate Army in August 1861. Within a year, Sheppard and his messmates, all members of Brig. Gen. Maxey Gregg's brigade of South Carolinians, found themselves deep in the swamps of Virginia's Peninsula south of Richmond, fighting not only Yankees but hunger and deprivation as well. Many were "barefoot, many more without a decent garment on their backs, more still ill with diarrhea and dysentery, and all half famished." Shot while fighting from an unfinished railroad cut at the Second Battle of Manassas on August 29, 1862, Sheppard died in a hospital camp at Warrenton, Virginia, three weeks later.

At Paris, Illinois, an Edgar County crowd says farewell as a new crop of volunteers leaves for the front in April 1862. The armies' need for fresh troops appeared insatiable. That same month the Union lost more than thirteen thousand men killed, wounded, and missing at the Battle of Shiloh in Tennessee. Confederates lost more than ten thousand in the same fight.

AARON WALCOTT

JOHN HORLE

For some Northerners, the shelling of Fort Sumter was a gauntlet thrown down. The attack so enraged Bostonian Aaron Walcott {left} that he enlisted in the 2d Massachusetts within two weeks of the event. "Wife did not take it very well, but she will think better of it one of these days," he wrote in his diary. "Country is everything." The former journalist and construction paymaster rose from private to senior first lieutenant, commanding a battery of artillery. At Gettysburg, his guns helped defend Little Round Top. After thirty-three battles, and with his three-year enlistment over, Walcott mustered out. Moving to Chicago, he sold real estate, worked in the storage business, and was a deputy sheriff before retiring at fifty-six. He died in 1907 in Massachusetts at age seventy-one.

German-born John Horle {right} came to the United States in the early 1850s. When the war broke out, Horle traveled from Buffalo to Pittsburgh seeking to join a Pennsylvania unit. Instead, he landed in a Union infantry regiment from what would later become West Virginia. As time passed, Horle's regiment became mounted infantry and eventually a full-fledged cavalry unit, preying on Rebel railroads and striking back at Confederate guerrilla raiders. Finishing out a three-year enlistment in June 1864, Horle was honorably discharged and given $12.44 due him from his clothing account, as well as a $100 bonus. After the war, he settled in Cleveland and raised a family there.

Above, center: Born in Europe, George and Herman Groth were Illinois volunteers. After American-born enlistees, German immigrants made up the largest group of Union soldiers.

Above: *A Rebel fiddler from Tennessee.*
Musicians like him played a key role in maintaining the esprit de corps of a regiment.

....

Opposite: *In Nashville, these handsome Tennessee artillerists,*
the Rutledge Rifles, arranged to have themselves photographed.
After the Battle of Shiloh, the war's first truly big fight,
they were consolidated with another unit.

THOMAS HERNDON

An illiterate, unskilled boy when he arrived in Tennessee in 1856, Thomas Herndon set out to improve his lot by trading work for food, lodging, and an education. His upward rise momentarily stopped by the war, he nonetheless enthusiastically enlisted for Confederate service with the 14th Tennessee, rising in rank to second lieutenant. Herndon took a bullet in the thigh at the Second Battle of Manassas in Virginia and recovered while his unit fought at Antietam in Maryland. The following summer, he was captured at Gettysburg and spent the rest of the conflict as a prisoner of war at Johnson's Island Federal prison on Lake Erie. Paroled in 1865, he returned to Montgomery County, Tennessee, made a fortune, then lost it in the crash of '93. He died a seasoned seventy-eight in 1917, the Manassas bullet still in his leg.

Above: *The fourth state to break away, Alabama seceded in January 1861, causing a wave of enlistment. Alabama Private J. F. Gaines poses in a Hardee-style hat.*

Left: *A well-equipped Alabama volunteer cavalryman in a photo titled "Jim and his Pony." Photographs of mounted Confederates are rare since most wartime Southern photography was done indoors, where expensive plates and chemicals could be economized.*

Below: *Shotgun-toting Alabama Pvt. O. T. Dozier. The weapons were often photographer's props.*

JOHN CASHNER JR.

Indianan John Cashner Jr. of Kokomo volunteered early in the war, fighting his first battle in June 1861 at Rich Mountain in western Virginia where, he confessed in a letter, he captured a fancy "pattent [sic] lever watch" off a Rebel and had to keep mum about it. In March 1862, his unit fought Confederate Maj. Gen. Thomas J. "Stonewall" Jackson at Kernstown, Virginia. Later, camped at Fredericksburg, Virginia, Cashner got to shake hands with President Lincoln, whom he described as "riding around the camp as common as any soldier." Cashner's military career ended in May 1862 when, suffering from dyspepsia and sun-strain, he was given an honorable medical discharge. After the war he hunted buffalo in the Dakotas, ran a drugstore, and peddled liquor. He died in Seattle in 1928.

JOHN GIBSON HERNDON

A seventeen-year-old Virginia schoolboy when he enlisted in 1862, John Gibson Herndon vowed to defend his home state from the Yankee "rain [sic] of terror and oppression on the east side of the Blue Ridge." After compiling an impressive service record with the Charlottesville Artillery in Stonewall Jackson's Army of the Shenandoah, Herndon transferred to the cavalry, which he found to be "full of exciting episodes and hazardous adventures. I had to be alert and always ready to fight in the saddle." Though wounded in summer 1864, he fought on until a second wound that November at Tom's Brook, Virginia, ended his service. Herndon lived out his life in Virginia, served as mayor of East Falls Church, and died there in 1928.

War was a family adventure.

....

Above: *The tasseled hats worn by North Carolina brothers William E. and Bennett Spach only seem to highlight their youth.*

....

Left: *Two stolid Rebel brothers proudly display crisp U.S. belts and buckles, most likely liberated from a captured Federal arsenal.*

....

Right: *Sidney and James Haight of the 1st Michigan Sharpshooters peer earnestly into a portrait-maker's lens.*

THE TOBIE BROTHERS

The war showed how strong individualistic streaks could be worn down. Raised in an idealistic abolitionist household, Leroy {left} and Edward Tobie—unlike most brothers on either side—enlisted in separate Maine units. Leroy finished his tour in May 1863 while Edward stayed on for the duration. If doubt that he had not fulfilled his duty nagged Leroy, especially when Edward, wounded at Brandy Station that June, was wrongly reported killed, he still resisted returning to the service, even when offered a quartermaster's position with another unit late in 1863. A year later Leroy finally rejoined the army. Though both men were wounded in the Appomattox campaign, older brother Edward's two wounds won him the Medal of Honor. After the war, the brothers went their separate ways.

CALVIN BURTON

A glance at the photograph of this sickly Alabaman dwarfed in an oversized uniform reveals a small, frail boy who looks much younger than his nineteen years. Calvin Burton had no business going to war, but the cure for patriotism is enlistment. Soon Calvin found himself in the 36th Alabama building fortifications around Mobile. Unable to keep up, Burton was discharged in less than eight months. The regimental surgeon blamed dropsy, or a severe accumulation of fluid in the abdominal cavity. Never really in good health, the would-be soldier died of tuberculosis at Greensboro, Alabama, in 1879.

WILLIAM HENRY HARRISON HUSSEY

A continent away from the fighting fronts, most California enlistees were assigned duty on the West Coast, but in October 1862 the governor of Massachusetts asked Captain J. Sewell Reed in San Francisco to recruit one hundred horsemen for service in the East. More than five hundred applied, but only the best were chosen. Although the unit was integrated into the 2d Massachusetts Cavalry, its members continued to wear the legend "Cal 100" on their forage caps, as shown in this photo of Lieutenant William Henry Harrison Hussey, a former gold miner and rancher who made the cut. Entering the war attached to Major General Philip Sheridan's Army of the Shenandoah, the Californians fought actions up and down the Shenandoah Valley, including the October 1864 Battle of Cedar Creek and skirmishes with famous Rebel raider John S. Mosby.

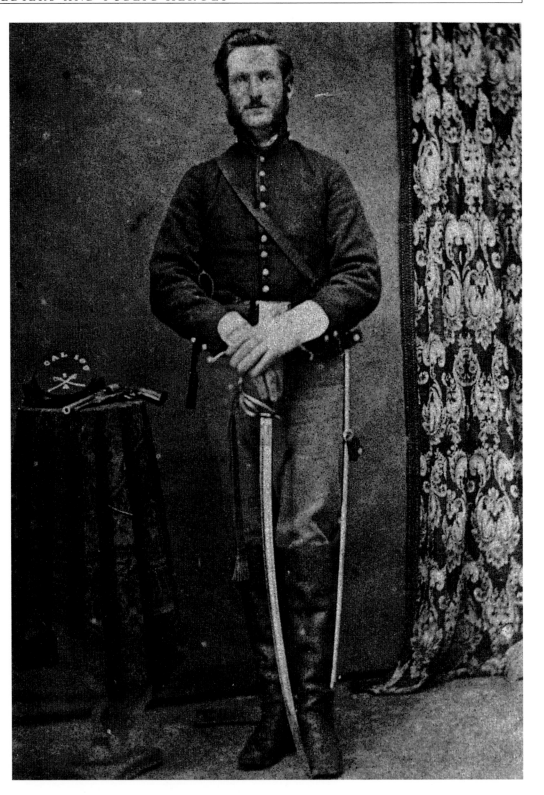

JAMES EMACK

GEORGE HENRY WILLIAMS

At the beginning of the war, soldiers often waited many months before seeing the enemy. Not so for James Emack, who signed on with the 7th North Carolina. It was March 1863, and the volunteers of the 7th were thrown straight into a war that was then at its height. At the Battle of Chancellorsville, Virginia, on May 3, Lieutenant Emack was one of five men sent to reconnoiter a confusing movement of Union troops that eventually became the wholesale surrender of the 128th Pennsylvania. It was during this confusion that Confederate Lt. Gen. Stonewall Jackson was mortally wounded by his own troops. The next day, as Southern forces continued to post a victory, Emack was killed in action. His death came less than sixty days after his enlistment.

George Henry Williams's mother made him wait a year until he was eighteen to join the Confederate army. All through 1862 he slogged along as an infantryman until, in 1863, he transferred to the cavalry after briefly considering joining the navy. That June, Williams, a Virginian, was engaged at Brandy Station in the largest cavalry battle ever fought on the North American continent. At one point, armed only with a saber, he captured a Federal soldier. While marching his captive to the rear, the Yankee produced a hidden pistol and shot Williams in the head, killing him instantly. He was buried on the battlefield, his grave marked by his brother James, an artillerist in the battle. James returned in August to remove George's remains to a family cemetery.

JAMES BALDWIN

James Baldwin was a runaway slave who, like more than 175,000 other African Americans, volunteered to serve the Union. At Wallace's Ferry, Arkansas, First Sergeant Baldwin and his cohorts of the 56th U.S. Colored Infantry held off a force of Rebels three times their strength for three hours until a Union cavalry detachment arrived to break up the Confederate line.

Baldwin was wounded in the neck during that 1864 engagement, spent three months in the hospital, then returned to active duty. At war's end Baldwin survived a cholera attack that killed 179 men in his regiment. An Arkansas farmer and drayman in peacetime, he retired to the National Home for Disabled Soldiers in Illinois, dying there in 1922 at the age of eighty-seven.

U.S. Colored Troops muster in at Delaware, Ohio.
This simple act was a triumph in itself. Even most white antislavery Northerners harbored the belief that black Americans would make poor soldiers.
The debate to allow their service did not conclude until July 1862.

IRWIN ELROY WARNER

The harsh realities of combat overwhelmed sixteen-year-old Connecticut volunteer Irwin Elroy Warner. Sleepy garrison duty around Washington, D.C., was no preparation for the grinding horror Warner faced when his unit was thrown into the spring 1864 Battle of Spotsylvania Court House, Virginia. Later that year Warner's Connecticut outfit helped repulse Confederate Lieutenant General Jubal Early's assault on Washington, D.C.

Private Warner deserted on July 18, 1864, six days after Early's foray. Ashamed of turning yellow, Warner volunteered for the Union navy under a false name. Although his true identity was eventually discovered, desertion charges were dropped. Warner served well beyond the war, being honorably discharged in 1867.

ALFRED COX SMITH

For some men, combat might have seemed preferable to the alternatives. Alfred Cox Smith fought in a Mississippi regiment until illness forced his resignation from the army in mid-1862. Once well, he sought to reenter the service but was advised by his brother-in-law, William Nugent, to reconsider. Nugent, a Confederate cavalry officer, urged Smith to avoid the war and take the family's womenfolk and slaves to Texas and safety. Was it the prospect of being cooped up with the women for the duration? Perhaps the women didn't want Alfred hanging around at loose ends. Maybe it was honest patriotism. In any event, the combative Smith—he was shot to death in an 1869 dispute—returned to finish out the war with the regiment.

Volunteers of the 9th Mississippi camping in pine flats near Pensacola, Florida, February 1861. One in a series of rare outdoor photos taken by Southern cameraman J. T. Edwards, this picture documents a situation similar to the one at Fort Sumter. These Mississippians were part of a force besieging a U.S.-held island fort in Pensacola Harbor, Fort Pickens. Reinforced, the Pickens garrison never surrendered.

CHAPTER II

COMMON SOLDIERS

WHO WOULD BE A SOLDIER? In America, in a society without castes, there once was a time when no gentleman, and no fellow who ever hoped to be a gentleman, would ever happily consider taking up army life. To be a common soldier was just that—common. If you came from a family of any consequence and took up "the profession of arms," if you became a soldier, it was believed both you and your relatives were in reduced circumstances. It was a Victorian-era embarassment. Soldiers were louts, losers, gamblers, and drunkards. In January 1861, only weeks before the start of the Civil War, the entire U.S. Army numbered just 16,367 officers and men, every one of them socially suspect to somebody.

While there was a stigma attached to serving, there was also a lot of hypocrisy. In the mid–nineteenth century, northern and southern boys were raised on the history and legend of George Washington, citizen soldier. The lucky ones with the time to study classical Latin and Greek were regaled with the story of the Spartans at Thermopylae, or of Horatio at the bridge. They were urged to read Julius Caesar's commentaries on his great campaigns. They were fed heroic yarns and tantalized with bawdy tales of military adventure. Then, as a caution, they were also reminded of something the Duke of Wellington was reputed to have said after his great victory over Napoleon at Waterloo. When asked what his common soldiers—his men—had contributed to his success, the elitist and incredulous Iron Duke supposedly said something like, "My men? Why, my men are scum."

Soldiers sat at the bottom of North American society, that is, until the great schism of 1861. Then, suddenly washed clean in a shower of patriotism, the profession of soldier was made decent. To be a soldier, defending the honor of your land, was moral, upright, a duty. It was

"in," it was all the rage, and at first it looked like fun. Bell Wiley, lauded author of two histories of Civil War common soldiers titled *The Life of Billy Yank* and *The Life of Johnny Reb*, wrote that early in the war the send-off and ceremonies heaped on troops in the rank and file made it seem like the life of a common soldier promised anything but misery. There were picnics and parades where volunteers were feted. There were identical ceremonies in the North and South where the women of the community made a flag by hand for the local volunteer regiment and all the girls turned out to present it to the men along with kisses on their bearded cheeks.

While it did suddenly become chic—or at least acceptable—to be a common soldier at the start of the Civil War, it definitely came at a price. In the Union army white privates were paid thirteen dollars per month, a paltry sum even by nineteenth-century standards. Black privates received only eleven dollars a month and were supplied with inferior weapons and equipment. In the Confederate army, a force backed by an unstable and inflated currency, privates received eleven dollars per month.

Young fellows who hailed from the southern aristocracy or from New England families of privilege found this pay scale made for rough going. In the early days of the war the folks back home sent them new clothes, custom-made boots and firearms, candies, liquors, and perhaps even a trusted family retainer or a loyal slave. When these moneyed boys served in elite regiments made up of fellows from the same class—outfits such as the 7th New York, made up of Manhattan society boys, or the Washington Artillery of New Orleans, a clublike organization comprised of southern social lions—these gifts from home caused no problems inside the army. When these same men were later brought into contact with a wide variety of volunteers and draftees, however, there was trouble.

Opposite: *Tiny Rhode Island, with less than 175,000 inhabitants, sent common soldiers like these four stalwarts off to war.*

Many regiments were raised in neighborhoods, counties, or communities where most of the men shared the same professions or trades or hailed from the same ethnic group. Consequently, both the Northern and Southern armies had entire regiments made up of firemen or woodsmen or coal miners or Germans or Irish or Jews.

In the upper-, middle-, and lower-class regiments, the men elected their own officers. As a result, as the war progressed, accomplished individuals representing all these classes, ethnic groups, and professions met as officers in planning sessions. Because of this, to a certain, creaky degree a very fragile form of egalitarianism started to move through the armies. Top to bottom, common soldiers realized that the success and survival of all the individual, segregated groups relied to some degree on the cooperation, success, and survival of the other individual, segregated groups.

In its way, war worked a leveling process on the common man in America, particularly if he served as a common soldier. North and South, the troops learned they all had the same general personal objectives. They wanted to survive the war, serve well, pick up a few good anecdotes, and go home to die in bed as content old men. They learned that these have been the goals of common soldiers in all times, in all wars. ✪

Above: *Three midwestern cavalrymen pose together.*
Farm boys made good horse soldiers.

....

Opposite: *These four brothers enlisted for the Union.*
They hold heavy-caliber hunting rifles.

An 1861 photograph of three Georgia boys: C. C. Taylor, J. D. Jackson, and a fellow named Porter.
With overcoats and scarves they look confident they'll be spending the winter above the Mason-Dixon Line.

A not so common-looking common soldier, Lt. Col. Thomas G. Woodward.
This informally dressed Kentucky cavalryman served with Rebel Brig. Gen. Adam R. "Stovepipe" Johnson, a plucky Confederate raider known to range as far north as Indiana.

Left: *A revealing early war photo of Confederate Col. J. V. Jordan wearing a Federal blue Mexican War–vintage uniform.*
In both North and South, common soldiers often went on campaign dressed for the last war, or in uniforms made by local seamstresses.
Center: *These pictures of Jordan were found in a photographer's shop in New Bern, North Carolina, by Union invaders in 1862.*
In this second photograph, it appears that by the time the Yankees arrived, Jordan, leader of the 31st North Carolina Regiment, had found a more modern cap.
But it was still a little too dark to be called Rebel gray. Standards weren't imposed on Union or Confederate dress until authorities decided the war would last awhile.
Down South, where cloth and braid were in short supply, those standards were rarely enforced.

..

Right: *The standard-bearer of the 108th U.S. Colored Troops. Common men, fellows who may have enjoyed no special position back home,*
found army life gave them opportunities to hold important ceremonial posts, including chances to stand—if only for a few minutes—out in front of the rest of the ranks.

..

Opposite: *Men of the 2d Rhode Island proudly pose for an action shot at Camp Brightwood near the Union capital of Washington, D.C.*
Poses like these allowed ordinary men a chance to play the part of heroes for the folks back home.

A stereo view of camp life: 2d Rhode Islanders and a servant at Camp Brightwood.

In Northern and Southern parlors
people used special viewers
to look at "stereopticons,"
or early 3-D photos such as this one.
Viewing stereos was considered entertainment,
and shots that put the viewer
in a military setting
were the most popular,
even when the pictures
showed battlefield destruction.
If anything, it prompted the parlor-bound
to look at their soldiers' lives
with a little more respect.

Above: *A steely eyed Mississippian, a common Southern soldier. Judging proportionally from his gun and saber, he was not a big man but average for the times. He and his fellow Mississippians would see their state overrun by armies for most of the war.*

....

Below, left: *Vicksburg, Mississippi, during the siege of 1863. From late May to July 4, Southern troops were trapped inside this riverside city without fresh rations or reinforcements. Virtually surrounded by well-supplied Union troops, the common Rebel eventually learned to survive on mule and rat meat. Their leader, Lt. Gen. John Pemberton, surrendered the city to Maj. Gen. Ulysses S. Grant on Independence Day 1863.*

....

Below, right: *Fort Hill, overlooking Vicksburg. Once a Confederate position, it was part of a miles-long system of Rebel trenches around the town. Lemuel P. Cosby {**opposite**} put in most of his time in a similar position called the 3d Louisiana Redan. Both Cosby's redan and Fort Hill were assaulted by Union troops who dug beneath them and set off large charges of gunpowder.*

LEMUEL P. COSBY

At the siege of Vicksburg, Cpl. Lem Cosby, 43d Mississippi, was sent with a detail to extend the Confederate line of entrenchments. When a hat carefully poked above the trench line was instantly perforated by a Yankee sniper's bullet, Cosby ordered the detail to fall out until after dark. Lt. Magnus L. D. Hodo, coming upon the napping soldiers, reprimanded Cosby and his men for being slackers. A heated argument arose.

"For every spadeful you dig, I'll dig two," Cosby hotly replied to Hodo's challenge, whereupon Lieutenant Hodo grabbed a shovel and stepped out into the open to dig. "Don't do it," Cosby warned the officer. Hodo was immediately felled by a Union bullet.

Lem Cosby endured the Vicksburg siege and most of his army's campaigns through 1864. He died an old man in 1921, having survived the war by having a foot soldier's common sense.

EDWIN AUGUSTUS OVERTON

Edwin Augustus Overton served a mere thirty days in Union army uniform in summer 1863, but they were an eventful thirty days. Sent to Pennsylvania with the 22d New York Militia, the handsome New Yorker found army life not much more than a grand camping trip, with time left over to flirt with nearby Susquehanna Valley farm girls. Then, on June 30, Overton's unit encountered a Rebel detachment at Sporting Hill, Pennsylvania, less than ten miles from the state capital, Harrisburg.

The Rebels in front of Overton were the vanguard of Gen. Robert E. Lee's army, probing ahead during what would become known as the Gettysburg campaign. At Sporting Hill a few shots were traded and both sides retreated. This was no grand battle. But it was the northernmost engagement of the war.

Overton's unit did not march to battle at Gettysburg. Instead, not long after the great fight, the 22d was rushed back to New York City to help quell draft riots there during July 11–13. Overton's brief but memorable first enlistment ended July 24. Family members say he reenlisted in a standard regiment and served out the war.

More New Yorkers:
Left: *Members of the 7th with their flags.*
This outfit was one of the most prestigious Empire State units,
raised in Manhattan and manned by many of the sons of the city's aristocrats.
It saw very limited service, and while fifty thousand New Yorkers died in service,
no man of the 7th was lost in combat.

Right: *New Yorkers of the 33d Infantry sit for the camera.*
The Empire State contributed more regiments to the Union cause
than any other state loyal to the Federal government:
474,701 New Yorkers wore Union blue.

JAMES JONES

Not many soldiers on either side could match the combat itinerary of James Jones {opposite}. Enlisting as a private in the 66th New York, from 1862 onward he fought in almost every major campaign of the eastern theater, including the Peninsula, Antietam, Fredericksburg, Chancellorsville, Gettysburg, Bristoe, Mine Run, the Wilderness, Spotsylvania, Cold Harbor, Petersburg, and finally the Appomattox campaign, where he witnessed the surrender of Gen. Robert E. Lee's army. He mustered out August 30, 1865, a first lieutenant with the 66th, at New York City, and vanished into history.

JOHN DAVID MYERS

Badly wounded at Fredericksburg, John David Myers was a lucky man. A tough South Carolinian from a storied unit, Myers belonged to Company D of the 3d South Carolina Volunteers of Kershaw's Brigade. Starting with the July 1861 First Battle of Bull Run, then the spring and summer 1862 Virginia battles called Seven Pines, the Seven Days, and Second Bull Run, Kershaw's men campaigned incessantly until December 13, 1862, when they found themselves occupying Marye's Heights at Fredericksburg. Myers's regiment was positioned on high ground not far from the stone wall, behind which other Carolinians fought from a position of comparative safety. Exposed on the hillside, 150 enlisted men and 18 officers out of 350 members of the 3d brigade died in the fight. Myers's wound at Fredericksburg kept him out of the war for a year, allowing him to miss the Gettysburg campaign, an operation that cost Kershaw's Brigade half its men.

Opposite: *The famed Stone Wall at Fredericksburg, Virginia.*
From colonial times, Fredericksburg thrived beside the Rappahannock River. Its waterside homes and businesses were backed by a slope called Marye's Heights. The stone wall ran along the slope's crest beside a sunken road. When Federals attacked the town in December 1862, they sent men marching toward Rebels packed three deep behind the protection of the stone wall. The Union lost 12,653 in combat for the town and in assaults on the wall. Comparatively few Southerners died in the fight.

WILLIAM DAY

Williams Day, a 54th North Carolina Infantry private, was typical of many common soldiers. A simple farmer, he despised fighting but would not desert, even when others did, even when one of his children died and his family needed him. Illiterate, he sent home a dozen dictated letters, each full of aching heartsickness. "I hope this war wil[l] pas[s] over without any more fighting," he wrote home shortly before the May 1863 Battle of Chancellorsville, Virginia.

The town of Fredericksburg, site of a great battle in December 1862, sat near the main Chancellorsville battlefield and was the scene of hard fighting during the Chancellorsville struggle. Day served on that Fredericksburg front in May and survived. But like many other Civil War foot soldiers, he succumbed to disease—in Day's case, typhoid fever—a month later.

An easy target for heavy Union cannon posted on hills across the Rappahannock, Fredericksburg was blasted apart in December 1862.
There Southern civilians came under intentional enemy fire for the first time.

CARL AUGUSTUS SCHWAN

Carl Augustus Schwan {opposite} was a sturdy Prussian immigrant from Wisconsin. (The man on the right is believed to be Schwan's friend Charles Schwartz.) A member of the 13th Corps, Schwan fought in western campaigns beginning with the siege of Vicksburg. The high point of his military career came when his unit, the 29th Wisconsin Infantry, was called upon to help free Union Adm. David Dixon Porter's fleet, marooned at Alexandria by low water.

Led by Lt. Col. Joseph Bailey, himself a former lumberjack, the midwesterners constructed a massive dam of logs to raise the water level of the Red River. On a signal, the dam would be breached and the fleet would wash through, passing over shoals. A first dam collapsed, but a stronger second dam worked, saving the vessels. Schwan's prairie farmer skill as a woodsman served his country well. He died at the age of eighty and was buried in Good Thunder, Minnesota.

Left: *The gunboat fleet of Union Rear Adm. David Dixon Porter stranded by low water on the Red River in Alexandria, Louisiana. Alexandria was one of the objects of a famous failed Union strategy, the spring 1864 Red River campaign.*

In early March Union Maj. Gen. Nathaniel Banks and Rear Admiral Porter set out from camps north of New Orleans to take Shreveport. Far short of their goal, Banks's soldiers were bloodied in battle at Pleasant Hill and Mansfield, Louisiana, by troops led by Confederate Lt. Gen. Richard Taylor. Then after occupying Alexandria, the level of the river dropped, stranding Porter's fleet and ending its support for Banks's men. The campaign faced disaster.

Right: *A log dam built by Union infantry outside Alexandria, the salvation of Porter's fleet. In places, the Red River was only four inches deep. The Federals managed to escape south through the building of this and another log dam, feats of engineering in which common soldiers such as Carl Schwan proved to be the keys to success.*

JAMES MONROE STOOKEY

Some men had an affinity for war. "I was never in any kind of business I liked so much as this," James Monroe Stookey once wrote his family. An able tactician, Captain Stookey was a firm but upbeat and considerate officer well liked by the men of the 59th Illinois. Stookey's soldiering stood out. Wounded at the September 1862 Battle of Perryville, Kentucky, he was cited for bravery at the year-end 1862 Battle of Stones River, Tennessee, and in the Atlanta and Nashville campaigns.

The often forgotten Battle of Stones River—or Murfreesboro—Tennessee, was a brutal experience for Stookey and the other men on these pages who counted it on their service records. Fought between Union Maj. Gen. William S. Rosecrans's army and troops led by Confederate Lt. Gen. Braxton Bragg outside the town of Murfreesboro and not far from Nashville, it took place December 31, 1862, and January 2, 1863. (The opposing armies used New Year's Day to rest and reorganize themselves.) It was effectively a draw, but Bragg withdrew his army from the field, allowing Rosecrans to declare the fight a strategic Union success.

An able company officer, Stones River survivor "Roe" Stookey was elevated to temporary command of the 80th Illinois Regiment at Atlanta and later of the 59th Illinois for the closing campaigns in the western theater. After the war, he returned to farming and family life, fathering five children before his untimely death at the age of forty-two in 1880.

LARKIN GERMAN

During the November 1863 battles for Chattanooga, Tennessee, twenty-six-year-old Larkin German and his fellow Confederates retreated from Lookout Mountain to Missionary Ridge, two heights overlooking the city. On November 25, while German and his comrades fought from the protection of a trench, a sniper killed his friend Osborn Davenport. German spotted a puff of the sniper's rifle smoke in a tree and promptly shot the Yankee. Later, he and Davenport's brother Garner were separated from their unit, stumbled into a Union camp, hastily fled into the woods, wandering until they found their regiment miles south of Chattanooga, near Ringgold Gap, Georgia.

German survived the summer and fall 1864 Atlanta and Nashville campaigns of the Army of Tennessee. At war's end, by then breveted a first lieutenant, German took a mule and an Enfield rifle back to Georgia, where he started life over again—this time with a wife, Mary Jane Davenport, sister of his old messmates Osborn and Garner.

JAMES T. McELVANY

Nobody knows what a man can stand until he tries it," Confederate Capt. James T. McElvany wrote his mother. "If I should fall, I can only wish to be in a better world than this, where the war whoops will not be heard and the weary are at rest."

Photographed in Richmond proudly displaying a shaved wound over his left ear, in 1862 McElvany and the 35th Georgia Infantry had already stood up to Virginia battles at Mechanicsville, Gaines's Mill, Frayser's Farm, and Cedar Mountain—where a shell fragment clipped him. Ahead of McElvany lay the Battle of Fredericksburg, the July 1863 Battle of Gettysburg (where his unit took part in Pickett's Charge), the spring 1864 fight at Spotsylvania, Virginia, and promotion to the rank of major.

The common soldier's other enemy—disease—finally got McElvany in February 1865. He ended the war in a hospital. Returning to Gwinnett County, Georgia, he and his father ran a successful clutch of shops. He died in 1901.

SAMUEL W. SUMMERS

War can seem to turn a man's luck. After an unsuccessful try at raising a regiment, Samuel W. Summers of Iowa, a wealthy and politically connected attorney, was handed the 7th Iowa Cavalry, a unit cobbled together from shorthanded companies by that state's governor on January 1, 1863.

Assigned to Fort Kearney, Nebraska Territory, Summers's command fared poorly. Responding to an Indian raid at Plum Creek Station, Summers's troopers took sixteen hours to travel thirty-two miles. By the time they reached the station the raiders were long gone. Embarrassed by that event, Summers pushed his horsemen far too hard on another occasion, pursuing Indian warriors into Colorado Territory. Arriving exhausted, the 7th was ambushed and fifteen men were killed. Summers was quietly discharged. After the war, he tried—and failed—at entering politics. The unlucky Summers died in a freak carriage accident in 1890.

Above: *Fort Berthold, Nebraska Territory. The common Union soldier served on the frontier as well as in the war-torn East.*
Most—from far Midwest states such as Kansas and Iowa—faced different problems and different hostilities "out there."
In this photo, Iowa troops are in peace negotiations with the Sioux. Conflicts with Native American tribes continued through the Civil War and after.

Below: *In the Dakotas in 1865, a Federal officer poses with Indian leaders. Out on the plains, this soldier's war rarely went well.*
He and his men were undersupplied and often neglected until there were civilian casualties or a military embarrassment.

Left: *The lone star on their hats marks these men as Texans.*
These are Shannon's Scouts of the 8th Texas Cavalry.
They took their frontier riding and fighting skills to battlefields in Georgia and Tennessee.

Many forget the Civil War was also fought west of the Mississippi River.
Both Union and Confederate armies called this southwest region the Trans-Mississippi.
War there attracted a different, independent-minded soldier. Some went east to fight.
Others stuck close, defending their homes, cotton, and cattle.

Above: *Many Texas Confederates were* vaqueros *who wore gray.*
In Laredo, from the left: Refugio Benavides, Atanacio Vidaurri, Cristobal Benavides,
and their friend John Z. Leyendecker. In the midwar years, Refugio Benavides commanded
a force that defended Laredo from invasion and beat back Union attackers.

JOHN M. BROWN

JACOB HEYER

Battles in the Trans-Mississippi were rarely glorious. That doesn't mean that the men who fought them were any less valorous than their eastern counterparts. John M. Brown of the 15th Texas is a fine example. Enlisting in March 1862, Brown brought years of rugged frontier experience—including skirmishes with Comanches—to his military service.

Brown was to fight in more than thirty small-scale but savage battles in the Trans-Mississippi, many of them in the watery bayous of Louisiana. In September 1863, Brown's Rebel unit was instrumental in capturing more than 450 Yankee prisoners at Stirling's Plantation near Morganza, Louisiana. During the Red River campaign, the 15th helped rout Maj. Gen. Nathaniel Banks's powerful army at Mansfield, Louisiana, the following spring. Brown survived war in the swamps and finished out his life in Texas, chasing Indians and outlaws.

Many soldiers remained in service throughout the war, glad to do what was needed for the cause. Jacob Heyer of Philadelphia enlisted as a private with the 23d Pennsylvania shortly after the attack on Fort Sumter. In 1862 his unit fought up and back down Virginia's Peninsula, south of Richmond, at Chantilly outside Washington, D.C., and at Fredericksburg. For his part in recapturing Marye's Heights during the May 1863 Chancellorsville campaign, Heyer earned the medallion seen pinned to his zouave uniform in this photo.

After serving as prison guards for a time at Johnson's Island on Lake Erie near Sandusky, Ohio, the 23d returned to Virginia in time for the disastrous June 1864 Battle of Cold Harbor and Grant's summer campaign in Virginia. By then Heyer was a captain. When the 23d disbanded in September that year, he reenlisted as a private, finishing the war with the 7th U.S. Veteran Volunteers.

Alexander P. Petrie

Entering the army along with his brother Edward in August 1862, farmer and future politician Alexander P. Petrie was soon recognized as a natural leader. Within a short time, Petrie was promoted to orderly sergeant then lieutenant in Company C, 112th Illinois Regiment. For a while, after being given horses, the unit served as mounted infantry. The brothers rode with Col. William Sanders on a successful raid into east Tennessee in the spring of 1863. By winter, however, the 112th had turned in their mounts and had reverted to being foot soldiers.

Assigned to the army's Atlanta campaign, the regiment stayed with Maj. Gen. William T. Sherman's forces from spring 1864 until the end of the war. At one point this meant detachment northwest for what became known as the Franklin and Nashville campaign. Edward Petrie was killed at the November 1864 Battle of Franklin, Tennessee. Alexander made it safely through the Battle of Nashville that followed, then helped pursue the defeated Army of Tennessee back to Alabama. After all that, Alexander Petrie was present when that same Rebel army surrendered to Sherman in North Carolina in April 1865.

Petrie went home to farm country where the votes of loyal veterans won him a place in the Illinois House of Representatives. He died in the town of New Windsor, Illinois, in 1898.

WILLIAM E. CHRISTIAN

Severely wounded at the July 1864 "Battle of the Crater" during the siege of Petersburg, Virginia, Sgt. William E. Christian of the 8th Michigan came perilously close to losing his livelihood, if not his life. Christian was on the Petersburg front when Federal tunnelers detonated eight thousand pounds of gunpowder beneath the Confederate trench lines. In the confusion after the blast, Christian's regiment was expected to charge through the breach the explosion tore in the Rebel defenses. Debris and bad leadership slowed the Yanks, however, allowing Confederate gunners to regroup and mass fire on them as they crossed the gap or "crater" created by the mine. A Rebel shell fragment splintered Christian's upper arm and sliced his biceps muscle to the bone. Miraculously, the arm was salvaged and Christian recovered completely.

Christian returned to his regiment and finished out the war, seeing no more combat. In peacetime he married, raised five children, and resumed his profession, one that required that mended arm. Christian was a portrait painter.

Opposite: *At Petersburg, after months of fearing the sniper's round, Union soldiers enjoy standing atop the trenches for a photographer after the April 1865 collapse of the Confederate defenses. The Union army invested Petersburg, south of Richmond, in June 1864. The siege lasted to within six days of Lee's surrender.*

JAMES H. KIERSTEAD

Chased across northern Alabama and tricked into surrender by Rebel Maj. Gen. Nathan Bedford Forrest, Indiana Col. Abel D. Streight's men figured they were headed for Libby Prison. Sergeant James H. Kierstead, one of Streight's soldiers, did not know how well he would cope in confinement, but he and his comrades knew what was to blame for their predicament. They blamed their mules.

When planning a foray across Alabama that would culminate with the destruction of the mills and factories at Rome, Georgia, it is said Union officers decided Streight's more than two thousand troopers could only make it across the great mountain ranges of northern Alabama on sure-footed mules. Only there aren't any great mountain ranges in northern Alabama. Hindered by the balky animals, Streight's men could never quite outrace the better-mounted men of Forrest, who intercepted them at Day's Gap and pursued them relentlessly until their surrender near Gaylesville.

Libby Prison was mainly for officers. Sergeant Kierstead was paroled within two weeks, but Streight stayed long enough to join in a remarkable escape from Libby in February 1864. For his part, Kierstead finished out the war faithfully, mustering out as a captain. On returning home he married and spent the remainder of his days as a pioneer in Nebraska.

Left: The former warehouse and ship chandlery of Libby and Son became Richmond's most famous prison. Not as infamous as Andersonville, the Confederate lock-up in Georgia, Libby Prison was still known as a place of hunger, crowding, and occasionally benign neglect. Some considered shipment there as something close to a death sentence.

Right: The interior of one Libby barrack hall. Many inmates claimed Union prisoners were packed so tight inside these unfurnished halls that when they lay down on the floor to sleep at night, they couldn't roll over unless they did so as a unit. Most of its inmates were Union officers.

JAMES MADISON CONAWAY

Common soldiers North and South wrestled with a lot of ambiguities. Not all their friends, relatives, and neighbors shared the same opinions about the war, and they weren't always sure who supported their decision to enlist. When thirty-year-old James Madison Conaway {opposite} signed on as a private in a Confederate battalion at Pollard, Alabama, in May 1863, he believed he was siding with the right. He discovered later he hadn't pleased everybody.

Conaway, then a father of three, posed proudly for the camera when he first went off to war. He wore a brass-buttoned, gray frock coat trimmed in blue and black, a feathered hat, and leather gauntlets, and he held up an 1841 Mississippi rifle for inspection. Then Private Conaway went off to serve in a Mobile, Alabama, garrison and later in the Rebel trenches surrounding Petersburg, Virginia. Things went downhill from there. On April 2, 1865, Union troops assaulted

Conaway's trench, took him prisoner, and tossed him into Maryland's Point Lookout Prison. Though the war in Virginia was over within a week of his imprisonment, Federal authorities would not release the Alabama private until he took an oath of allegiance to the United States government.

If James Conaway felt he was suffering an injustice, a family member disabused him of the notion. A slaveholding cousin from Delaware, Curtis Conaway, wrote to James in prison: "Why dount you take the oath of a legents [allegiance] to the goverment and git out? It is rite you should do it. The South had no bisoness of soseding at furst. It is the worst thing she ever don for her self. The common class is to be pitted [pitied] but the ledors aut to be hung as hy as havon."

Private Conaway took the hint, swore the oath on June 10, and went home to Alabama, where he farmed and served as a justice of the peace. He died there at age sixty-six, the father of a total of ten children.

Left: *A pleasant-looking Alabaman, Col. W. H. Swan hailed from the state that raised the first half-million dollars to finance the new Confederate government in 1861.*

Center: *The popular Napoleonic pose, this time struck by Capt. Eddie Crenshaw of Alabama.*

Right: *Alabama Pvt. T. P. Larkin's photo reflects the young man's seriousness. While his home state was overwhelmingly pro-Confederate in sympathy, it did harbor pockets of strong pro-Union sentiment. It took flexibility on the part of young common soldiers like Larkin, and old familial and fraternal ties, to keep the domestic peace.*

CHAPTER III
UNCOMMON
MEN

UNCOMMON MEN

IF THEY WERE NOT FAMOUS, if they were not leaders of armies, and if they were not common soldiers, who were those fellows who stood out from the dull ranks of blue or gray, the ones with odd jobs or unusual status or quirky accomplishments or who committed one lone act of bravery? Here we call them the uncommon men, a catchall phrase to describe the individuals who gave the story of America's Civil War some of its color. They could be grouped into some broad categories. But out of the millions who had a hand in the great war of the 1860s, there were many more characters than there were written parts.

For example, armies on campaign attract more than just soldiers. During the Civil War there were people who looked at the troops passing by and saw money and opportunity on the march. Some of those people were called camp followers: civilian cooks, laundresses, prostitutes, and peddlers. Others were uncommon men who had interesting civilian occupations: journalists, photographers, and newspaper illustrators. Still others, such as professional intelligence men, had jobs no one cared to talk about. They were spies.

War and army life also attract people hungry for experience. During the Civil War, this meant women, youth, and people of color—folks who up to that time had been customarily denied a taste of life's zest—had a chance to grab a thrill or make their mark if they seized the opportunity. They put on disguises, lied about their ages or backgrounds, and took off to get in on the action. Their adventures captured the imaginations of Americans in the 1800s, making real-life heroes out of some very ordinary people. One of them was Johnny Clem of Ohio, a nine-year-old runaway who served as drummer boy for a Michigan regiment, survived the Battles of Shiloh and Chickamauga, then, on the strength of his service, continued in the army until retiring at the rank of major general in 1916.

Beside these innocents stood some people with unusual talents and special abilities that in any other period might have made them criminals. In peacetime these uncommon men might have been accomplished thieves, liars, or smugglers; in time of national emergency, however, and in the official record, they were patriots. One who won fame for his slippery wartime talents was Virginia attorney John S. Mosby. He organized several bands of partisan rangers, or Confederate guerrillas, that operated in and around the Blue Ridge Mountains, robbing Union supply trains, raiding towns, and kidnapping Union officers. He practiced what might now be considered commando tactics; then they were called something close to banditry. Mosby was simply the best-known warrior of his type. There were others who practiced his brand of warfare, but they didn't have his flair for publicity.

For whatever reason, at some point cameramen had a chance to photograph a sampling of these uncommon types. Most were forgotten. Mid-nineteenth-century Americans were focused on record-holders, the unusual, the extreme. Most of the Civil War's uncom-

Opposite: Sutlers, men whose business it was to retail commodities to soldiers in the field. Operating with government permits, they followed campaigning troops providing what the army didn't furnish—from writing paper to candy, woolen mufflers to liquor, bologna to oysters. Above: Sutlers like A. Foulke were part of a civilian "army" that trailed behind the soldiers. When armies settled near big cities like Richmond or Washington, the sutlers, cooks, laundresses, prostitutes, photographers, adventurers, clergymen, politicians, and other hangers-on could outnumber the soldiers two to one.

mon men didn't meet the criteria for tabloid celebrity that still holds today. They were not the largest, the smallest, or the first. Those Civil War–era records went to fellows such as the twenty-four-year-old member of the 192d Ohio who stood just three feet four inches tall or to Confederate Maj. Gen. Leonidas Polk, the only Episcopal bishop in uniform, or to Maj. Martin Delaney, the first black man commissioned as an officer in the U.S. Army, or to David Van Buskirk, at six feet ten inches the tallest American soldier, or to Loretta Velasquez, a Louisiana woman who claimed to be the first of her gender to wear a disguise and serve as a Confederate officer.

Most of the forgotten uncommon men did make a contribution, however, to their country or their profession or their cause or—in a few cases—to literature. For decades, their letters and diaries and reports have proven to be good resource material for historians, and some of those who wrote memoirs helped inspire at least one genre, the espionage novel. Allan Pinkerton, founder of the National Detective Agency, helped establish the U.S. Secret Service and popularized the term "private eye." During the war he served as Union Maj. Gen. George McClellan's chief of intelligence and established a spy network in the upper South. Later he wrote several melodramatic memoirs about his Civil War adventures, naming names, and revealing, often for the first time, the identities of some uncommon men who took professional pride in being unknown or forgotten, the uncommon men modern readers call secret agents. ✪

Above: *War correspondents demonstrate conviviality around a punch bowl. A few of the war's uncommon men, they were present at some of its great battles and helped write history. In those years, however, most newsmen had a political point of view which colored every dispatch from the field. For this reason, they were despised by most generals. When told that a correspondent had been killed in a recent battle, Union Maj. Gen. William T. Sherman is reputed to have said, "Good. Now we shall have news from Hell before breakfast."*

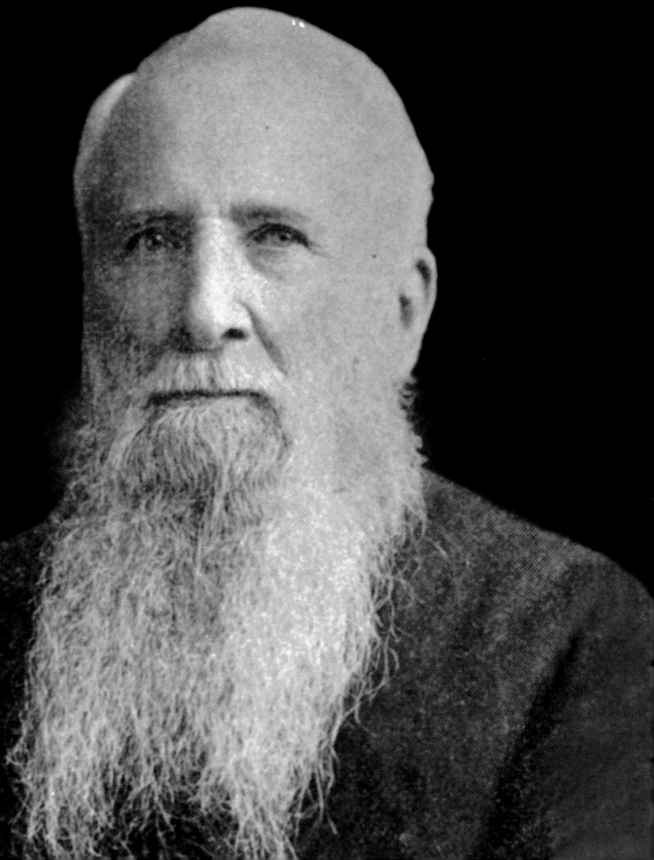

As a soldier-turned-chaplain,
Milton Haney never quite lost his taste for a fight.
A Methodist minister, Haney captained the 55th Illinois,
was twice cited for bravery, rose to the rank of colonel
and command of the 55th, yet resigned his commission
in 1864 to serve out the war as regimental chaplain.
Still, when finding himself trapped in a trench
at the Battle of Atlanta, Georgia, in 1864,
the Reverend Haney picked up a rifle and fought
like a foot soldier, even leading a counterattack
when his commanding officer was killed.
Haney's combativeness bought time
for a Union rally that saved the day.
Writing years later about his wartime experiences,
Haney commented, "a chaplain who is all head
and no heart is a miserable makeshift."
Apparently, Haney was a man with
an uncommon degree of heart.

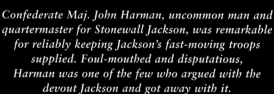

Confederate Maj. John Harman, uncommon man and quartermaster for Stonewall Jackson, was remarkable for reliably keeping Jackson's fast-moving troops supplied. Foul-mouthed and disputatious, Harman was one of the few who argued with the devout Jackson and got away with it.

Uncommon man Luther Swank is not remembered for his work as a hospital orderly in Pickett's division of the Confederate army. Instead, this inveterate letter writer is recognized as one of the great amateur chroniclers of the war. In dozens of letters to family and friends, Swank reported on everything from troop movements and battle results to the inflated prices of beef, flour, and potatoes in war-torn Richmond. Observant and perceptive, Swank just liked to write about the things going on around him. His letters were rich in detail, such as the comment that some wealthy refugees in Richmond wore evening finery because everyday clothes had been sold for food or rent. Historian Douglass Southall Freeman frequently used Swank's letters as source material in his own Pulitzer Prize-winning work two generations later.

Uncommon man and unusually good provider Billy Crump of the 23d Ohio, a legend within the Union army for his foraging skills. As an aide to Col. (future U.S. President) Rutherford B. Hayes, Crump once went alone into the West Virginia countryside for two days and returned with fifty-three fowl, twenty dozen eggs, and thirty pounds of butter. Like all good army scroungers, Crump probably never admitted the food was stolen. Some foragers did pay civilians for food, but the usual rule was finders-keepers.

Some uncommon men weren't men at all, but women.

Above, left: *Born in Ireland, Jennie Hodgers lived out her whole life as a man. She enlisted in the Union army as Albert J. Cashier in 1862 and served until the South's surrender. Her gender was not revealed until a doctor uncovered her secret following an automobile accident in 1911.*

Above, right: *Pvt. Franklin Thompson was actually Sarah Emma Edmonds, a Canadian who enlisted in the Union army in 1861. In disguise, she served two years then, after falling ill, deserted before her deception could be detected by a doctor. After the war, Edmonds married a man and raised a family. Following the publication of her memoirs, she was admitted into the Grand Army of the Republic, a Union veterans organization. Thompson is believed to have been the GAR's only female member.*

LAMAR FONTAINE

Lamar Fontaine was one of the most remarkable personalities of the Civil War—if you believe Lamar Fontaine. A self-proclaimed explorer, engineer, poet, crack shot, and doer of daring deeds, this Confederate major may also have been the war's champion liar. Fontaine claimed to have been captured by Comanches as a child, fought in the Mexican War, sailed to Japan with Commodore Perry, and been decorated by the czar for bravery in the Crimean War.

During the Civil War, he claimed to have suffered sixty-seven wounds. From Jackson, Mississippi, Fontaine smuggled secret messages—along with eighteen thousand percussion caps—to besieged Rebels at Vicksburg, traveling first on horseback, then on foot, and finally in a dugout canoe floating under the noses of Yankee gunboats. At least that was Fontaine's version of his war experiences. That he died in 1921 at age ninety-two is an established fact. The rest of Fontaine's career is delightful conjecture.

WILLIAM CECIL PRICE

Missouri politician William Cecil Price was an outspoken pro-slavery Democrat, a man of such uncommon devotion to the principles of the Southern cause that he quit the post of treasurer of the United States in the administration of President James Buchanan to throw in with the Confederacy.

Though an important politician, Price apparently had little military aptitude. Captured at the March 1862 Battle of Pea Ridge, Arkansas, then paroled and finally shuffled off to train recruits, the unhappy firebrand resigned from Confederate service in 1863. But he never disavowed the political position that led him to leave the U.S. government. When Price died in 1907, the Springfield, Missouri, newspaper eulogized there had been "perhaps no man in the United States who held on so tenaciously to the ideas of a vanished political and social age."

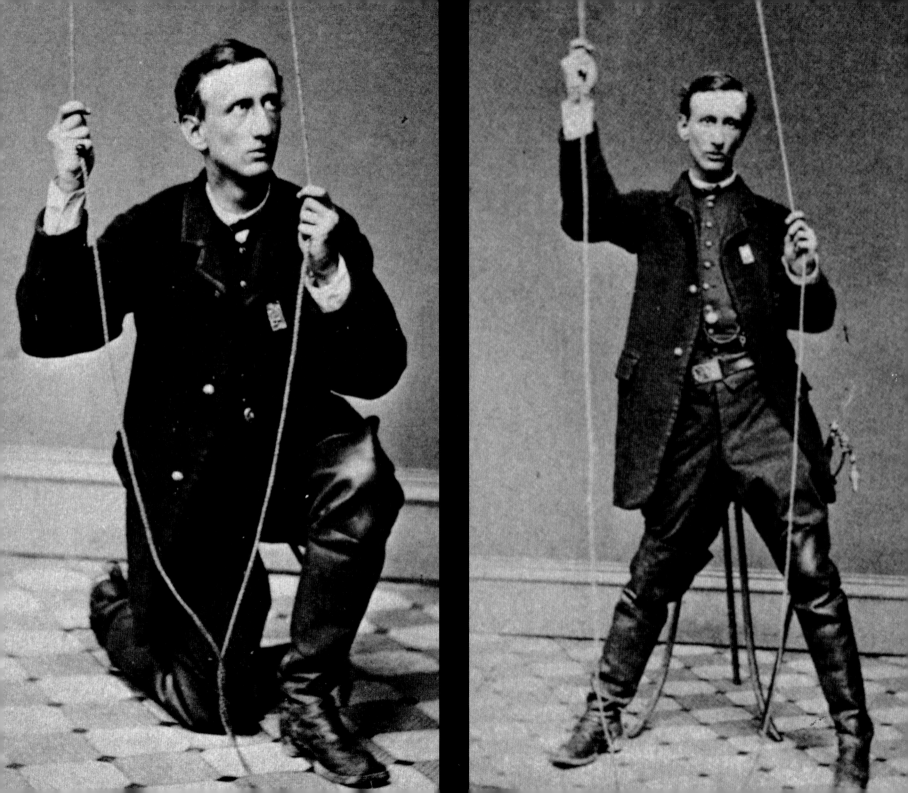

JOHNSTON LIVINGSTON DEPEYSTER

Lt. Johnston Livingston DePeyster, eighteen years old, climbed to the roof of the Confederate capitol early on the morning of April 3, 1865, and raised the first U.S. flag flown over Richmond in four years. Son of a Union general, DePeyster was an unusually ambitious young man. At sixteen, he recruited more than fifty men for the 128th New York Volunteers, but was not allowed to join them due to his youth.

After serving with the 7th New York Militia during the New York City draft riots in 1863, he was commissioned a second lieutenant in the 13th New York Heavy Artillery, the unit he was serving in when he made his bold dash to the roof of the Virginia statehouse, flag in hand. The young man was widely celebrated as a Northern hero. DePeyster had these photographs made several years after the war to commemorate his moment of glory.

Above, left: With Richmond in ruins at war's end, the U.S. flag flies from atop the captured Virginia statehouse. The photo had great emotional appeal to Unionists, and so did the story of how the flag was planted there by a young soldier named DePeyster.

Above, right: When Richmond fell, many Northern personalities were photographed standing in front of the Virginia statehouse, which had served as home to the Confederate congress. In this shot, uncommon man and famed photographic entrepreneur Mathew Brady is himself seen wearing a tall hat and standing on the left side of the group.

ELIJAH WHITE

JOSEPH PIERCE

Sold for six dollars in Canton, China, to New England sea captain Amos Peck in 1852, cabin boy Joseph Pierce grew up in Hartford, Connecticut, and was reared and educated like the other Peck children. Going to war ten years later, Pierce may have been the only Chinese in the Union Army of the Potomac. He served in the eastern theater with the 14th Connecticut, the most battle-scarred of that state's regiments, and mustered out a corporal at war's end.

Taking up silversmithing as a trade after the war, Pierce married Martha Morgan and had three children. When he died in 1916, the local paper made no mention of his race, instead stating simply and appropriately that Pierce was "well known and liked."

If not a celebrated soldier, Elijah White was certainly not average. Enlisting as a private in the 7th Virginia Cavalry, "Lige" White would rise to the rank of lieutenant colonel by war's end. At the October 1861 Battle of Ball's Bluff, Virginia, he personally led a small group of Confederates in capturing 325 Union prisoners. Recommended for promotion but with no commissions available, White was given the opportunity to raise his own regiment of partisan rangers. "White's Rebels," an outfit combining the qualities of guerrillas with those of mounted commandos, fought throughout the war attached to the Army of Northern Virginia.

Steady, dependable, and tough, White was wounded twice but never put out of action. Following the war, he settled back into civilian life as a farmer, a banker, and later as a sheriff.

HENRY BROWN

In this uniquely American conflict, sometimes the expected patterns didn't apply. Henry Brown was a free black, a talented brickmason who served not the North but the South. A drummer with the Darlington Guards of South Carolina, Brown was apparently the only regularly enrolled African-American member of Confederate forces raised in that state. Despite ample opportunity during the tumult of war, Brown had no interest in fleeing the Southern side for political freedom in the North or a position with the Union army's black troops.

After the war, Brown entered politics, winning office during Reconstruction, then used his position to help his old Confederate comrades. At his death in 1907, the otherwise all-white membership of his unit gave Brown an elaborate military-style funeral, then erected a monument in his honor.

In 1990, the people of Darlington, South Carolina,
restored this 1907 monument to uncommon man Henry Brown.

ANDREW J. INGALLS

Some soldiers stood out because they were the best at something. This was especially true of approximately twenty-five hundred Union soldiers who qualified to join Berdan's Sharpshooters, elite sniper units organized by national rifle champion Hiram Berdan. One of the snipers was this man, Andrew J. Ingalls, a stalwart New Hampshireman with a steady hand and a clear eye.

To become a member of the Sharpshooters and earn the unit's distinctive green uniform, a Union soldier had to place a bullet within five inches of the center of a ten-inch target, shooting ten shots "off hand" from one hundred yards, then ten more "at rest"

from two hundred yards. Ingalls was enrolled in Company G, 2d U.S. Sharpshooters, serving from August 1862 until his 1864 capture near Petersburg, Virginia.

After six months' captivity Ingalls was released in a prisoner exchange and allowed to go home for a thirty-day leave. While recuperating from his prison ordeal, he posed for this photograph. In it he is wearing the plain blue uniform given to returned prisoners of war. The sniper then went back to the Virginia front and served through the Appomattox campaign. Following his June 19, 1865, discharge he made his home in Laconia, New Hampshire.

Above: *With its heavy barrel and tube scope, this muzzle-loading sharpshooter rifle was accurate at distances up to a half-mile. The item protruding from the barrel is a detachable plunger that was struck with a mallet to drive a tight-fitting bullet all the way down to the weapon's breach. Among one group of uncommon men, this rifle was considered the most deadly of weapons.*

J. P. GRINSTEAD

Who was the youngest commissioned officer in the Union army? J. P. Grinstead of Kentucky imagined himself to be that man, enough so that he staked his claim to that title in a letter to the *National Tribune*, the official newspaper of the Grand Army of the Republic, a Union veterans organization. Grinstead wrote in great detail about his entry into the army as a fifteen-year-old. Rising from private to first sergeant to regimental commissary sergeant, Grinstead was a participant in the western theater Battles of Shiloh, Corinth, Perryville, and Stones River.

In January 1863, Grinstead was promoted to first lieutenant. He was seventeen years, five months old. By that fall, just past his eighteenth birthday, he was promoted to captain of Company H of the 9th Kentucky. Grinstead's claim is unverified, but in his wartime photo, the brave youngster—wounded three times—wears an officer's coat.

PRYCE LEWIS

Pryce Lewis was an Englishman who used his accent and a natural talent for deception to spy for the North. Working for famous detective Allan Pinkerton, Lewis traveled western Virginia posing as an English lord, complete with a manservant, fancy clothes, and a two-horse carriage. Lavishing cigars and champagne on unsuspecting Rebel officers, Lewis obtained valuable information that led to the summer 1861 Union capture of Charlestown, in what is now West Virginia.

On a later mission to Richmond, Virginia, Lewis was not so lucky. Recognized on the street by some people he had duped, Lewis was imprisoned and scheduled to hang. Eventually, Confederate leaders let him go, figuring him for a small fish. Though his exploits then and later became the subject of pulp novels, Lewis ended up penniless. A showman to the last, Lewis committed suicide at age eighty-three by leaping from New York City's Pulitzer Building.

HENRY THOMAS HARRISON

The Confederacy produced no more enigmatic spy than Henry Thomas Harrison. Originally from Mississippi, Harrison's undercover work attracted the attention of Confederate Secretary of War James Seddon who eventually assigned the spy—or scout, as he was called—to Lt. Gen. James Longstreet shortly before Lee's Army of Northern Virginia made its way into Pennsylvania in June 1863. It was Harrison's report that Union Maj. Gen. George G. Meade had crossed the Potomac River in search of Lee's army that altered the course of the Pennsylvania campaign.

Longstreet immediately sent Harrison to Lee's tent with the report, and Lee changed his plans as a result. The armies would collide accidentally at the little town of Gettysburg, Pennsylvania, but Lee would not be caught unawares.

Ironically—considering they relied so heavily on the man's word—no Southern officer knew the spy's first name or his true occupation. Perhaps that's a tribute to Harrison's espionage professionalism. But in this lighthearted photo, he breaks with it just a little, holding up for some dear one the coded message "I Love You."

LAWRENCE ORTON WILLIAMS

Military justice was swift and unsympathetic for Lawrence Orton Williams. Posing as Federal military inspectors passing through Tennessee, Williams—a Confederate colonel and first cousin of Gen. Robert E. Lee's wife—and Lt. Walter G. Peters were detained by suspicious Union officers at Fort Granger outside the town of Franklin. When their cover stories didn't add up, a quick "drumhead court-martial" was held, and the two were promptly hanged.

While Williams did not question his sentence, neither would he admit to being a spy. To this day, no one knows what his mission really was. This photo of him in civilian dress is all we have. No image of him in any uniform is known to exist.

THOMAS JEFFERSON PRICE

Some uncommon soldiers found themselves fighting under two flags. Cap-tured Confederate troops were often given the option of remaining prisoners of war or of pledging allegiance to the Union and joining its military. Not every Southern patriot's resolve was diehard, certainly not that of Thomas Jefferson Price, a Mississippi boy captured a few days after the Battle of Gettysburg.

Photographed here as a Confederate, after capture and acceptance of Federal service, this "whitewashed Rebel" was assigned to the 1st Connecticut Cavalry and sent to Minnesota on frontier duty for the remainder of the war. One of more than six thousand Rebels who switched sides, Price would later recall that enduring the harsh winters of the upper Midwest was every bit as challenging as facing enemy bullets.

His decision to switch sides apparently did not make him persona non grata back in Mississippi in postwar years. He settled there, raising ten children before dying in 1900.

THOMAS JEFFERSON WILLIAMS

Some uncommon men served on the fringes of the war. At age fifty, too old to be conscripted, Thomas Jefferson Williams avoided Confederate service at the start of the war, then in 1862 he raised a regiment to fight against the Confederacy—despite being a planter, slaveholder, and prominent Arkansas businessman. A ramrod-tough Tory, Williams saw action in the Trans-Mississippi first as a Union scout and spy then later as an irregular and informer in Conway County, Arkansas, his home.

A man like that makes enemies. Sixty Rebel cavalry surrounded his home one winter night in 1865 and assassinated him in front of his wife and children. Williams went down with guns in both hands.

MICHAEL USINA

Here is the portrait of a wanted man. Union naval officers had copies of his photograph. One Yankee officer could even identify his voice. Michael Usina {opposite} was wanted because he was one of the South's best blockade-runners—daring sea captains who darted up and down the coast and across the seas smuggling vital supplies into the Confederacy.

A Savannah, Georgia, river pilot before the war, Usina started his service as an infantryman because the South had no real navy in 1861. A wound at the First Battle of Bull Run in Virginia put Usina out of action for half a year. By then, the Confederate navy had taken shape, and he put in for a transfer. Ultimately, Usina would captain a series of blockade-runners with names like *Atlanta*, *Armstrong*, *Rattlesnake*, and *Whisper*. He was never captured. When the Confederacy collapsed, Usina sailed to England, relinquished command of his vessel, then returned to Savannah and a quieter life as a river pilot.

Usina captained ships like the Confederate blockade-runner Robert E. Lee.
Formerly a British vessel called the Giraffe, *the* Lee *had a runner's typical build. Low-slung, narrow-hulled, and steam-driven, these swift boats featured collapsing funnels and just enough sail for mechanical emergencies. Captured and refitted by the Union, the* Lee *was renamed the* Fort Donelson *in honor of a famous 1862 Northern victory.*

Shiloh was a two-day affair.
Confederate Brig. Gen. Adley Gladden was
wounded on the first near a hard-fought-for bit
of ground called the Hornet's Nest, its bullet-
pocked landscape shown above.
After shell fragments tore into one of Gladden's
arms, the limb was amputated on the field.
He died two days later.

ADLEY GLADDEN

Adley Gladden was a war hero, but not of the Civil War. He served with distinction in the Mexican War of the 1840s. A prosperous South Carolinian, Gladden had moved to New Orleans by the early 1860s. When his old home state seceded, he briefly commanded the 1st South Carolina Volunteers before returning to Louisiana to engage in secession politics. As the war got under way, the veteran soldier led Louisiana troops to Pensacola, Florida, to join Gen. Braxton Bragg's Rebel army then besieging Union-held Fort Pickens out in the city's harbor. Bragg recognized the fifty-year-old Gladden's ability and groomed him for higher command. Before he could prove his worth, however, Gladden fell at Shiloh. His death in that battle was overshadowed by the loss of the more famous Confederate Gen. Albert Sidney Johnston, killed in the same fight. That Gladden—a competent soldier, promising leader, and successful businessman—died as forgotten as the fallen footsoldiers who served him and others is why he is remembered here. These are believed to be two of the three photos of him known to exist.

Maj. G. S. Whipple Surgeon
13th Reg Ky Cav C.S.A.

DR. GEORGE S. WIPPLE

In wartime, one man can make a big difference in the lives of the soldiers around him. Dr. George S. Whipple was an assistant regimental surgeon who served the Confederacy with the 4th and 13th Kentucky Cavalry. Originally from Massachusetts, Whipple taught school as a young man to pay his way through the University of Louisville, where he studied medicine.

Slightly built but big in spirit, the little doctor was the heart of the regiment. Recognized as a good surgeon, Whipple also assumed the role of friend and counselor. The men turned to him in times of depression, bad news from home, or grief at the loss of a comrade. He was always approachable. "There were other physicians," a fellow cavalryman wrote after the war, "but they were not endowed with that sympathetic magnetism which characterized Doctor Whipple."

Whipple soldiered on through the end of the war then went into private practice in Louisville. On his death in 1881, his obituary noted Kentucky veterans were "always loud in his praise."

OVID WELLFORD SMITH

Ovid Wellford Smith {opposite} was only seventeen when chosen to be part of the Andrews raid. En route south across Tennessee to join Andrews at Marietta, Georgia, Smith and his partner, Samuel Llewellyn, claiming to be Kentucky Rebels, were picked up by Confederate patrols. The delay caused the two men to miss the raid. When Llewellyn ran away, the Southerners, suspecting Smith all along, threw him into Swims Prison in Chattanooga with the rest of Andrews's by-then-captured raiders. Because Smith and the other raiders gave no sign of knowing each other, Smith probably avoided a noose.

Smith later escaped Swims, rejoined his Ohio regiment, and served out the war, often acting as a scout or spy. Though recommended for the Medal of Honor along with the other raiders, he never received the award. In Columbus, Ohio, in 1868 Smith died of pneumonia at age twenty-three.

Probably the most famous locomotive in any war, the General {**above, center**} *was a central character in the famous Andrews railroad raid of April 1862. Covert Union operative James J. Andrews and twenty-four army volunteers dressed as civilians—traveling in small, separate groups—infiltrated Confederate lines. As passengers they boarded a northbound train at Marietta, Georgia, then hijacked it and its locomotive the* General *near Kennesaw, above Atlanta.*

Above, left and right: *The destruction of vulnerable wooden bridges like these between Atlanta, Georgia, and Chattanooga, Tennessee, were the objects of Andrews's raiders, but they were pursued by Confederates aboard the locomotive* Texas *and captured. Andrews and seven of his men were hanged. The rest later escaped prison or were exchanged. Ovid Smith played a forgotten part in the drama.*

CHAPTER IV

SACRIFICES

OST TRUE WAR STORIES ARE SAD ONES, and in long, patriotic wars that number of sad stories grows very large. In those wars soldiers fight for their homes and their beliefs, not for land or booty. The soldier's cause is sacred. Almost every loss is sanctified. Sacrifices are expected.

In the Civil War more Americans lost their lives, their health, or their property than in any other conflict the nation has had. In cash, it cost the North more than three billion dollars to conduct the war from 1861 to 1865. By 1879 — when pensions, liability claims, interest on government borrowing, etc., were figured in — it had topped six billion dollars and was still growing. At the turn of the twenty-first century the equivalent value of a billion Civil War–era dollars is awkward to calculate. Six billion, however, was a staggering sum.

The very existence of the Confederate States of America must also be considered a cost of the war — if no one had formally organized a Rebel government, there probably wouldn't have been much of a fight. From 1861 to 1863 it cost more than two billion dollars just to operate the Confederate government. If complete records existed, it might be calculated that it cost the defeated South nearly as much cold cash as it did the North just to take the issue to the battlefield. This loss to Confederate patriots does not, however, include private Southern real estate given up to the U.S. government after the war in lieu of unpaid taxes—the crisis Scarlett O'Hara faced in *Gone with the Wind* when the tax bill was laid on the family plantation, Tara. It does not include the destruction of the infrastructure, lost railroads, destroyed bridges, burned public buildings. It does not include the collapse of the South's agricultural economy. It does not include heartbreak.

About a year after he gave his Gettysburg Address, praising Union troops who fell in that battle, President Abraham Lincoln was credited with writing something scholars call "the Widow Bixby letter." It was reprinted in Northern newspapers and widely circulated. It is now believed that it was written by a Lincoln political partisan or administration staff member, and research has failed to verify the existence of a Widow Bixby. The sentiments in the letter, however, are pure Lincoln. The losses it refers to were suffered by many mothers.

November 21, 1864

Dear Madam:

I have been shown in the files of the War Department a statement of the Adjutant General that you are the mother of five sons who have died gloriously on the field of battle. I feel how weak and fruitless must be any words of mine which should attempt to beguile you from the grief of a loss so overwhelming. But I cannot refrain from tendering to you the consolation that may be found in the thanks of the Republic they died to save. I pray that our heavenly Father may assuage the anguish of your

Opposite: *Union army sick and wounded, Ward K, Armory Square Military Hospital, Washington, D.C. Most casualties never saw the inside of a place as clean and tidy as this.* **Above:** *William Denny of the Twenty-ninth Pennsylvania wears a coat with an empty sleeve. Denny lost his right arm in the summer 1863 Battle of Resaca, Georgia, north of Atlanta. Near the end of the war he took part in a "left-handed penmanship" contest, a national competition organized to help recognize the self-rehabilitation efforts of disabled veterans. This photo documenting his loss accompanied his contest entry.*

bereavement and leave you only the cherished memory of the loved and lost and the solemn pride that must be yours to have laid so costly a sacrifice upon the altar of freedom.

Yours very sincerely and respectfully,

Abraham Lincoln

How much did American soldiers and citizens give during the Civil War? A standard regiment—when it was first organized—was expected to hold as many as a thousand men or more. In many regiments, when men were lost from the ranks they were not replaced and the size of the unit shrank. At the Battle of Antietam in September 1862, the 1st Texas—in service less than a year and a half—was only able to field 226 men. Of those, 186 were killed or wounded in the battle, a loss of more than 82 percent. The 1st Minnesota went into the July 1863 Battle of Gettysburg with 262 men. Only 38 came out alive and unhurt.

Between 1861 and 1865 more than one million Northern and Southern men in uniform were killed, wounded, lost in action, slain by disease, crippled, disfigured, blinded, or made insane through war service. One hundred sixty-seven Union soldiers were shot for desertion. More than twenty-six thousand Confederates died in Northern prisons. In excess of forty thousand Northern soldiers came down with typhoid or similar fevers. No one kept figures on the number of children this war orphaned, how many widows it made, or how many futures it ruined. Sacrifices were expected. ✪

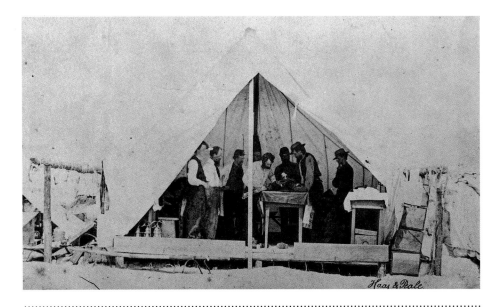

Above: *A Union army surgical tent, Morris Island, South Carolina, July 1862.*
Anyone carried out of combat alive ended up in a similar field hospital. Union and Confederate physicians treated the wounded of both sides, but many reserved the best care for the men of their own army.
Opposite: *On the Antietam battlefield, September 1862, Louisiana troops lie dead behind the weak cover of a fence along Maryland's Hagerstown Turnpike. Their sacrifice speaks to the futility of war. Estimates of Union and Confederate killed, wounded, and missing in this one-day fight exceeded twenty-six thousand. The battle was a draw.*

Above: *An unidentified recuperating Confederate officer with his crutches,
his sacrifice documented by the Richmond photographic firm of Charles R. Rees & Co. around the year 1863.*

Opposite: *Phoebe Yates Pember. A well-to-do young Southern widow, she migrated to Richmond, Virginia, from Georgia to care for sick and wounded
Confederates and to serve as chief matron of Hospital No. 2 in the sprawling capital-area tent-and-cabin army medical facility called Chimbarazo Hospital.*

Below: *Chimbarazo Hospital, Richmond, Virginia. Phoebe Pember's 1879 war memoir,* A Southern Woman's Story, *described it as
a place manned by incompetent doctors and bureaucrats. Supply shortages intensified the suffering there.*

Not everyone let a wound keep him out of the fight.

....

The soldiers pictured here are unidentified members of the Union army's Invalid Corps.
Later renamed the Veteran Reserve Corps, it was an outfit made up of slightly disabled soldiers who declined discharge.
Members wore sky blue uniforms (which make them appear gray in some black-and-white photographs).
They were armed with revolvers since some were missing a hand or fingers or an eye,
losses that made the standard muzzle-loading rifle of the time awkward for them.

....

Above right: *A one-armed officer of the Invalid Corps.*
He and his men were assigned light guard or escort duties or watched over prisoners of war.

EDWARD BLAKELY

When Edward Blakely posed for this photograph, he was not aware that he had been born too soon. He became a soldier before the development of rehabilitation programs, decent prosthetics, or the creation of psychiatry. He served in combat more than fifty years before the U.S. military first set up care for disabled veterans.

Born in Britain, Blakely worked a farm near Beverly, Ohio, before enlisting as a corporal in Company D, 63d Ohio Infantry, on October 9, 1861. He served as a teamster or wagon driver throughout his service and was rarely near the action. On July 21, 1864, at Decatur, Georgia, however, he and the rest of his outfit's drivers came under Confederate artillery and small arms fire. Union artillery returned the fire and covered the teamsters as they tried to escape up a nearby road. In his flight, Blakely was hit above the right elbow by a Southern rifle shot. The bullet shattered the bone. In a tent field hospital Union surgeons amputated the corporal's arm.

Blakely recuperated then mustered out November 11, 1864. He went home to discover that a one-armed farmer faced a tall wall of obstacles. In this era when nothing on a farm was automated, everything depended on the individual strength and stamina of the man who worked the land. He could not cope and on October 18, 1867, took his own life. Uncounted numbers of Union and Confederate veterans came to the same end. They decided for themselves that the sacrifice asked of them was too great.

Sixty-four percent of Southern war deaths were attributable to disease.

....

Above, left: *Andrew Jackson Read of Calcasieu Parish, Louisiana. Not long after the Civil War broke out he crossed the state line and joined Company F,*
5th Texas Volunteer Infantry. He was nineteen years old. By September 1861, he was in camp in Richmond, Virginia, and by early December was ill with typhoid fever.

....

Above, right: *Lt. Pryor L. Bryan of the 5th Texas, another native of Calcasieu Parish.*
He attended to sick Private Read and bore the duty of writing the boy's family after he died of fever in a camp in Prince William County, Virginia, on December 19, 1861.
To Read's sister Jane, he wrote: "I do assure you that there is no accident that ever occurred to this regiment that could of hurt me worse than his death.
I felt like I was loosing a close friend. He was one that was universally liked by all that became acquainted with him....Miss Jane I will say this to you that there has not
been one man in this whole regiment that has been sick that has had better attention and nursing than he had had." Lieutenant Bryan had done much of the nursing.
Bryan himself died a little more than four months later in a private home in Virginia. It is not known whether his death was due to wounds or disease.

EDWARD T. COLLIER

Some volunteers never had a chance to seek glory. One of them was Edward T. Collier of Massachusetts. In May 1861, an emergency call for troops resulted in the citizen soldiers of the 3d Massachusetts Militia being rushed off to Fort Monroe, Virginia, with less than a day's notice. Several men in the outfit were left behind in Boston; there simply had not been enough time to contact all the members. While those left behind waited for transportation and reorganization, Edward Collier decided to throw in with them. He enlisted on July 1, was issued a hodgepodge uniform scrounged from various Boston depots and private sources, then sometime later sat for this photograph. It is one of the few things that documents his service.

Collier's outfit was redesignated the 1st Battalion Massachusetts Infantry, and he was shipped off to Fort Monroe, a fortress sitting between approaches to Hampton Roads and the swamps of Virginia's Peninsula. A few weeks of summer service in this climate laid Collier low. He died of typhoid in Fort Monroe's Hygenia General Hospital on September 8. It is quite likely that he never saw an enemy soldier, let alone fired a shot at one.

JOHN AND JACOB BREON

These are the Breon brothers of the 36th Iowa Infantry, John {standing} and Jacob {seated}. Their family made a great sacrifice. There were four Breon brothers in Union service. One, Christian Breon, was captured and housed in Georgia's infamous Andersonville prison. Another, Joseph Breon, was captured then lost in the records. He is believed to have died in captivity.

Twenty-eight-year-old John, a husband and father of three, and twenty-four-year-old Jacob joined Company H, 36th Iowa Infantry on August 11, 1862. Most of their service was in Arkansas under Brig. Gen. Frederick Steele. In

Steele's spring 1864 Camden expedition, a strategy to lure Confederates away from the Red River region, John and Jacob Breon served in engagements at Elkin's Ford, Prairie d'Ann, Jenkins Ferry, and Camden, then were captured defending a Union wagon train at Marks's Mill on April 25. They were marched promptly south, covering a phenomenal fifty-two miles in twenty-four hours without food or rest. Nineteen days later they reached Texas and the Camp Ford prison pen. There, in July, Jacob died of unknown causes. In August, John died of chronic diarrhea, contracted from poor sanitation facilities.

Union veterans of Camp Ford, a prisoner-of-war lock-up four miles northwest of Tyler, Texas.
They posed for these shots in Louisiana after release at the war's end.

Ford was one of the healthier Southern POW camps. It had a source of pure water, and food supplies were adequate.
Inmates manufactured handicrafts and sold them to Tyler-area locals. Their straw hats, all made by inmate labor, shielded them from the harsh Texas sun.
Crowding, however, was a problem and increased the incidence of disease. At its busiest, Ford held forty-nine hundred captured Union officers and men.
In summer 1864 most of its inmates were picked up during the Red River campaign in Louisiana.

FANNIE JACKSON AND MARTIN BUSHNELL

This is Fannie Jackson of Georgia {opposite, seated} and her family in the postwar years. In summer 1864 Mrs. Jackson and her children were displaced from their Snake Creek Gap property, north of Atlanta, by campaigning Union troops. Her husband was away serving in a Georgia state regiment. Interestingly, though Mrs. Jackson's husband served in a Confederate unit and she lost her home to U.S. soldiers, both were Union sympathizers. Fannie took up work as a nurse in the general hospital of the Union's Army of the Cumberland in occupied west Georgia.

Meanwhile, Cpl. Martin Bushnell of the 154th New York {above}, campaigned past the site of Mrs. Jackson's Snake Creek Gap home and fought in the May 1864 Battles of Resaca and New Hope Church. He was shot in the right leg in a fight at Kolb's Farm, Georgia, on June 24.

The lower part of Bushnell's leg was amputated and complications set in. A surgeon in the Army of the Cumberland's general hospital was a distant relative of the corporal. He asked nurse Fannie Jackson to take him under her personal care. She moved Bushnell into her hospital apartments and over weeks brought him back to health. His condition finally stable, he was sent north in the autumn. The nurse and patient never saw one another again. In 1866, Bushnell died from complications from his old war wound. Mrs. Jackson was contacted and asked to write his epitaph. She wrote, in part, "Sleep on our loving brother, sleep....This marble shall thy memory keep...." She named her youngest child Martin, in honor of the lost Union veteran.

MINOR MILKEN

Col. Minor Miliken of the 1st Ohio Cavalry looked every bit the cavalier in this photograph. In keeping with the image, he died a cavalier's death. Just twenty-eight years old, through autumn 1862 Miliken led his regiment on a number of hunts for famed Rebel cavalry leader John Hunt Morgan of Kentucky. Then, late in the year, on duty with the Union's Army of the Cumberland, Miliken's men rode into middle Tennessee and on December 31 took part in the battle of Stones River.

Confederate cavalry assaulted the rear of the Union army during this fight, and Miliken and his men were ordered to drive them off. After charging the enemy, the colonel found himself in a classic saber duel with Southern swordsmen.

Accounts state he was finally overwhelmed by numbers then shot by an unchivalrous Confederate. Union Maj. Gen. George H. Thomas wrote Miliken's family: "While mourning his loss, you have the consolation of knowing that he fell a Christian and a patriot defending the honor of his country."

JOHN B. KING

ANDREW RUSSELL DENTON

This is the Reverend John B. King. A forty-one-year-old clergyman, King declared "I have been preaching for peace much of my life, and now I'm going to fight for it." He then entered the 10th New York Volunteer Cavalry on December 16, 1861.

Within a year King rose to the rank of second lieutenant. With his unit he served in most of the major eastern campaigns of the period, then on June 9, 1863, was in the saddle for the Battle of Brandy Station. Near the end of the fight, Union cavalry charged Confederate horsemen occupying Fleetwood Hill, a key position of the battleground. Lieutenant King never reached the top of the hill. His left arm shattered in the firing, he was captured by Confederates and sent to Richmond's Libby Prison. After weeks of misery in prison, his arm was amputated at the shoulder. Ten days later, on July 31, he died. Asked on his deathbed if he had a last message for his family, King replied, "Yes. Tell them I died like a Christian and a soldier."

In this photograph Andrew Russell Denton holds a small Bowie knife and tries to adopt a serious expression for the camera. A native of the Knoxville region, he had just enlisted in the 43d Tennessee and within a month would marry local girl Martha Palmer. Very few happy times came after that.

Denton's outfit, assembled in December 1861, was shifted around Tennessee until it was pulled into Gen. Braxton Bragg's September 1862 invasion of Kentucky. Denton got through that experience then was assigned duty in Vicksburg, Mississippi, around December. A little more than five months later the town was under siege, and Denton was under fire.

Denton was shot June 22 and died four days later of what was believed to be blood poisoning. His family line, however, survived the war that claimed his life. On November 8, his young bride, Martha, gave birth to a son, Hulbert Webb Denton.

MICHAEL CORCORAN

Here stands Michael Corcoran of New York {**fourth from left**}, one of the Civil War's colorful characters, and members of his staff. Born in County Donegal, Ireland, Corcoran immigrated to the United States in 1849, became involved in New York City affairs, and by 1859 rose to the colonelcy of the 69th New York Militia, a state organization dominated by Irish-American volunteers. He narrowly escaped court-martial for refusing to parade his Irishmen before the visiting Prince of Wales in 1860, and the next year led the regiment into the Civil War and combat in the First Battle of Bull Run.

Corcoran was captured at Bull Run, was later exchanged, and returned north a hero, rallying Irish-Americans to the Union cause and organizing the 155th, 164th, 170th, and 184th New York Regiments. This collection of regiments was dubbed the Corcoran Legion, and Corcoran himself was made a brigadier general.

Though an inspiration to his Irishmen, Corcoran had a reputation as a carouser. While serving as a division commander at Suffolk, Virginia, in 1863, he was returning from a late night with friends when he shot and killed an officer of the guard. Though he claimed the shooting arose from a misunderstanding, the killing of the officer, Maj. Edward Kimball {**next spread**}, tainted Corcoran's reputation. On the night of December 22, 1863, while returning from a drinking party, Corcoran fell beneath his horse and was crushed to death by the animal.

EDGAR KIMBALL

B oth the man and dog in this photograph would soon know heartbreak and tragedy. Lt. Col. Edgar Kimball of the 9th New York Volunteer Infantry, a noted citizen of New York City, went off to war with this pet, its name now lost to posterity. Kimball fought in North Carolina at Hatteras Inlet in August 1861, at the Battle of Roanoke Island the following February, in the 1862 Battles of South Mountain and Antietam, Maryland, and in the Battle of Fredericksburg, Virginia, in December. His dog waited for him back in camp during every fight. Then came what was supposed to be a quiet posting to the conquered town of Suffolk, Virginia.

In the dark hour before dawn on April 12, 1863, Kimball was serving as an officer of the guard outside his army's Suffolk camp. A group of officers approached and, questioned at a distance, did not know the countersign or password. Official reports record that Kimball, with sword and pistol drawn, made threatening moves toward the group. He was shot by the group's ranking officer, Brig. Gen. Michael Corcoran.

There were official inquiries, official regrets, a near-mutiny by the late Kimball's troops, then a long ride to New York City where the lieutenant colonel was laid out at City Hall. In all the tragedy, no sight moved the mourners more than that of Kimball's dog, still with him, waiting loyally beneath his coffin.

JOHN MOY

John Moy, of west-central Wisconsin, was photographed two to three weeks after he and his companions distinguished themselves in the Battle of Gettysburg. Moy was an immigrant from Canton Bern, Switzerland, who moved to Wisconsin in the early 1850s. On May 10, 1861, Moy enlisted in the Buffalo County Rifles, a Wisconsin unit raised by John Hauser, a Swiss Military Academy graduate and professional soldier. It is said when Hauser first saw his men clumsily go through drill, he remarked they looked "yust like one damn herd of goose." This was the source of the outfit's nickname, "Hauser's Blond Gooses."

Moy and the Blond Gooses were folded into a famous outfit called the Black Hat Brigade, after the tall, black hats the men wore, or the Iron Brigade. From the August 1862 Battle of Groveton during the Second Bull Run campaign through to the end of its service, the Iron Brigade fought through all the Army of the Potomac's major battles.

Moy came through the Battle of Gettysburg, but on May 12, 1864, during one of the Union's horrific assaults on the Confederates' fortified lines at Spotsylvania Court House, Virginia, he was mortally wounded. He died the following day and was buried in what is now Fredericksburg National Cemetery.

Below: The Gettysburg battlefield, site of the most famous fight of the Civil War and the largest battle ever fought in the Western Hemisphere. Literally thousands of stories of heroism and sacrifice came out of this one collision of armies. Among them was the valiant fight of Wisconsin troops on the first day of the three-day battle. In a counterattack on Confederates in a railroad cut there, they captured the flag and most of the men of the 2d Mississippi Regiment.

Above, left: *Seventeen-year-old Cadet Pvt. Thomas G. Jefferson of the Virginia Military Institute.*
At the May 15, 1864, Battle of New Market in the Shenandoah Valley of Virginia,
hard-pressed Confederate Maj. Gen. John C. Breckinridge was forced to commit 258 boys from VMI to the fight.
At day's end, Breckinridge defeated Union Maj. Gen. Franz Sigel's numerically superior force, but not without heartbreak.
There were several losses among the institute cadets. One was Private Jefferson, mortally wounded.

*And some were lost before the main event. Lt. George Busch {**above, right**} of the 98th Pennsylvania was maneuvering with his troops*
in the early days of the Chancellorsville campaign when he was killed by Confederates
outside the town of Fredericksburg, Virginia, on April 30, 1863. The Battle of Chancellorsville was fought May 2 and 3.

ROBERT GRIER MACAULAY

This is 1st Lt. Robert Grier Macaulay of Company I, 7th North Carolina Infantry. At age twenty, he enlisted in his company in August 1861 and with it campaigned along the North Carolina coast and fought in the Seven Days' Battles, the Battle of Cedar Mountain, the Second Battle of Bull Run, and the Battle of Antietam.

Macaulay's company found itself serving under Brig. Gen. James H. Lane in the Battle of Chancellorsville. On May 2, 1863, the men found some abandoned Union trenches along the battlefield and moved into them. Not long after, a column of Northerners tumbled up to the works, intent on manning the "vacant" stronghold. Finding Macaulay's troops there was a surprise, and unprepared to fight, the Federals surrendered. There were no easy victories the next day.

On the morning of May 3, Lane ordered the 7th and 37th North Carolina Regiments to charge up Chancellorsville Hill to "drive the vandals from their works." They succeeded, but the 7th lost 127 men wounded and 37 killed. Lieutenant Macaulay was among the wounded. On May 7 he died at Guinea Station, Virginia, en route to a Richmond hospital.

THOMAS Y. BENNETT

By birth and trade, Thomas Y. Bennett {opposite} should never have found himself posing for this farewell photograph. Bennett belonged to a special old Yankee breed. He was a native of Massachusetts's Nantucket Island and a seaman by profession.

The firing on Fort Sumter moved twenty-three-year-old Bennett to enlist in Company C, 2d Massachusetts Infantry on May 25, 1861. The unit was not fully equipped and uniformed, so when the sailor sat down to have this durable tintype made he wore a military vest under a civilian frock coat, held a pair of blue-tinted "sun goggles" in his hand, and showed off a handkerchief sticking from his coat pocket. It is all we have to remember him by.

With the 2d Massachusetts, Bennett campaigned in the Shenandoah Valley and faced Stonewall Jackson's troops there and at the Battle of Cedar Mountain in 1862. Then, serving with the army's 12th Corps, tumbled into the Battle of Antietam. Shortly after 7:00 A.M. on September 17, Bennett's unit was called to plug a breach in the Union line and brace a tenuous position near the Confederate-held Hagerstown Turnpike. There, the 2d Massachusetts charged across farmer David Miller's cornfield into a hail of bullets and shells. The men strained to reach the fence between the cornfield and turnpike, but the enemy fire was unbearable. Bennett the sailor was one of the dead the 2d Massachusetts left on the field.

Above left: This is some of the carnage on the Antietam battlefield, one in a series of scenes captured by Northern photographers. The images eventually circulated in both the North and the South, stunning civilians. It is widely known as the bloodiest day in U.S. military history; more Americans were lost in that fight than were lost in the World War II D-day invasion at Normandy.

Above right: A field hospital on the Antietam battleground. Although Union Maj. Gen. George B. McClellan's army and Lee's forces fought each other to a standstill on September 17, 1862, Lee believed his army's position was not tenable, and he withdrew from the field. As they retreated across the Potomac into Virginia, most of his regiments were forced to leave their badly wounded comrades behind.

Not all the best-remembered photographs of combat casualties came out of famous battles.
This shot was taken the day after the May 19, 1864, Battle of Harris Farm, Virginia,
by independent photographer Timothy O'Sullivan.
He is believed to have arranged most of the bodies in ways that enhanced his shots.

GEORGE WASHINGTON LOOKADOO

This is Cpl. George Washington Lookadoo of the 34th North Carolina Infantry, holding what looks to be a percussion-cap boot pistol and an outsized Bowie knife, probably made at a local forge near the town of High Point.

The improbably named Lookadoo hailed from North Carolina's Rutherford County, and at the time of his 1861 enlistment in a local outfit named the Sandy Run Yellowjackets, he was married to Julia Ann Lookadoo.

The Yellowjackets were eventually incorporated into the Confederate army as Company C, 34th North Carolina Infantry and set to duty guarding the state's coast. In spring and summer 1862 it took part in all the Army of

Northern Virginia's major campaigns then, following their defeat of the Union army at the Second Battle of Bull Run, attacked the enemy rear guard on September 1 in the Battle of Chantilly. In that fight, on a site that is today not far from suburban Washington, D.C., Lookadoo suffered a gunshot wound to the left arm. He was evacuated to Richmond, where his condition worsened. On November 3, the corporal was pronounced dead of "traumatic erysipelas and supperative fever"—nineteenth-century medical jargon for complications from his battle wound. He left behind his widow, Julia Ann, and a daughter he had never seen, eight-month-old Martha Ann Washington Lookadoo.

WILLIE GROUT

Eighteen-year-old 2nd Lt. Willie Grout {opposite} of Company D, 15th Massachusetts Volunteer Infantry, the only son of a prosperous Bay State family, was photographed in a moment of safety and pride in the town of Worcester, Massachusetts. He entered the army in June 1861. He was back in Worcester within six months.

In 1860 Grout entered Worcester's Highland Military School and there showed a natural proficiency in military tactics. He rose to captain of cadets and when the Civil War broke out was persuaded to serve as a civilian drillmaster. Young Grout, however, wanted to go into the army and had to plead for weeks to get his parents' consent. When he won them over, he entered the 15th Massachusetts and taught new recruits how to drill. Col. Charles Devens, the 15th's commander, called Grout "a model of behavior."

The 15th Massachusetts was part of a seventeen-hundred-man force that crossed the Potomac near Leesburg, Virginia, on October 21, 1861, with orders to scout the area and take Leesburg if possible. On crossing, the Federals scaled Ball's Bluff and there met about four thousand Confederates. The Massachusetts troops took casualties as soon as the fight opened, and Grout was delegated to ferry some of them back across the Potomac in a flatboat. Returning from his crossing, he found the ground below Ball's Bluff covered with bodies. Confederates above were firing down on Federals cowering among the rocks. When Grout asked Colonel Devens what was to be done, Devens said, "Nothing but take care of yourself."

Grout tried to swim 150 yards to nearby Harrison's Island but was shot in the head. His body was dragged from the Potomac November 5 and buried in Worcester by his devastated family on November 12.

Above: Col. Edward D. Baker, former U.S. senator from Oregon,
prewar political ally of President Abraham Lincoln, and one of the Union's first celebrity casualties.
On October 21, 1861, he led a reconnaissance in force across the Potomac to the heights above the river called Ball's Bluff,
not far from the town of Leesburg. His troops were met by men of Confederate Brig. Gen. Nathan G. Evans's command
and blasted back to the river, in some cases literally forced from the cliff top to the rocks far below.
Baker himself was killed early in the fight. Many others tried to swim across the Potomac to safety and were shot in the water.
The gruesome results of this reconnaissance brought on a congressional investigation.

Not all sacrifices were blood sacrifices. In some, land and property were lost. In this photograph, Southern civilians are being sent on the refugee trail by occupying Union forces. With her wagon filled with children and all her worldly possessions, the matriarch standing beside the load, wearing a sunbonnet and clutching a pipe in her teeth, still looks tough and resilient.

JOHN FIELDING MILHOLIN

J ohn Fielding Milholin posed for this photograph in 1861 at age twenty-nine sometime after joining a Georgia unit called Phillips' Legion, an organization made up of an infantry battalion, an artillery battalion, and a cavalry battalion. A former court clerk and schoolteacher, the husband of Lucinda Eveline Milholin, and the father of six children, he rose to the rank of captain in the legion's cavalry then was killed on a scouting mission in Virginia on November 10, 1863.

That was not the end of Captain Milholin's service, however. The next year Union Maj. Gen. William Tecumseh Sherman's armies passed through Milholin's hometown of Cassville, Georgia. His widow hid several of the captain's effects—his sword and pistol among them—and ran from her home with her children. Marauding Yankees burned their house to the ground. For some time the canopy over her husband's tomb provided Lucinda's children some shelter. Later she sold the captain's books to buy a cow; she converted his old uniforms into clothes for her boys. Other articles of John Milholin's effects were sold to give his family a new start. Fortunately for the family and the historical record, the widow never parted with his photograph.

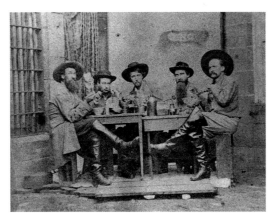

Above: *Captured members of Confederate Brig. Gen. John Hunt Morgan's cavalry,*
incarcerated in Pennsylvania's Western Penitentiary outside Pittsburgh. Most Confederate captives were kept in stockades in large numbers.
Slippery individuals such as Morgan's raiders, men who once ranged into Ohio, got special consideration and were securely locked up.

Below: *A more typical circumstance for Confederate prisoners was this setting, Camp Morton, outside Indianapolis, Indiana.*
Here the men were literally penned in, and their only shelters were flimsy, crowded shacks and barrack-like long houses.

CHARLES STEVENS

Not everyone wanted to be a soldier. This is an 1860 photograph of Charles Stevens of Savannah, Georgia, a Danish immigrant, and his five-year-old daughter, Mary Henrietta. In 1864, at age forty-eight, he was pressed into active military service and made to bear the burden of Confederate defeat.

Stevens came to America in 1835 and by 1840 had established a small business in Savannah shipping crops to other southern ports. By 1862, the war locked up Savannah Harbor, and Stevens's business foundered. By 1863 he was made a member of a local militia unit, an outfit composed of men too old or too young to serve in the regular Confederate service. The next year the government decided men between ages seventeen and fifty were fit to serve, and Stevens's militia was incorporated into Company I, 29th Georgia Cavalry. This unit skirmished with Union troops as they approached Savannah. Then on December 22, 1864, the day after the city fell to the Federals, Stevens and seven other Confederates trying to reach Rebel lines were captured by Union sailors.

Stevens, the immigrant Confederate conscript, was locked up in a stone-block bastion called Fort Delaware near present-day Rehoboth Beach. Conditions there proved to be the end of him. He died in captivity on February 1, 1865.

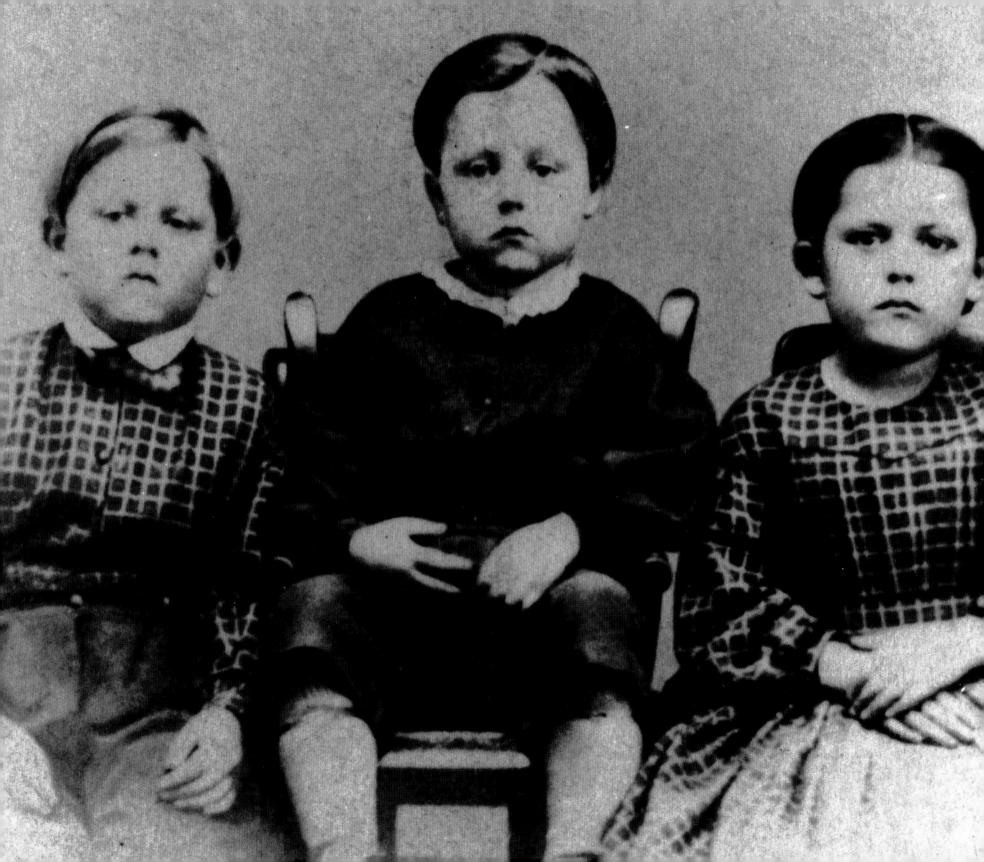

The Children of Sergeant Humiston

These are the children of Sgt. Amos Humiston of New York State. Their father's sacrifice and their loss moved the Union. After fighting passed through the town of Gettysburg, July 1, 1863, a Union burial party found an unknown Union sergeant lying on Stratton Street. In his hands he clutched this photograph. Even the hardened burial detail was moved by the scene. They saved the photograph, marked the spot where they laid the sergeant to rest, then told others of what they had found. News reporters heard the story and added the sad little tale to their pieces to give them some strong human interest.

The pathos in the scene moved Northern newspaper readers. A Philadelphia doctor had thousands of copies of the photo circulated throughout the North, hoping to find out who these fatherless children were. The search for the sergeant's family was successful. When a copy of the photo made its way to upstate New York, investigators were informed the dead man had been Amos Humiston; his widow was Phylinda, and his children's names were Fred, Frank, and Alice. Then those who helped in the search took their work one step further; they sold photos of the children to help fund the establishment of an orphanage in Gettysburg. The widow Humiston was its first matron and Fred, Frank, and Alice its first residents.

The home for soldiers' orphans, Gettysburg.

STEPHEN P. CATLIN

This is Stephen P. Catlin, a forty-four-year-old carpenter from Farmington, Illinois. When he enlisted in the 123d Illinois Volunteer Infantry on September 6, 1862, his wife and three daughters were fearful. Stephen's twenty-year-old son, Clinton, had enlisted in the 8th Illinois and been killed in the April 1862 Battle of Shiloh. His other son, George, just fifteen, was serving with the 5th Illinois Cavalry. If Stephen were hurt or killed, what would become of the family?

Catlin the carpenter felt the need to go. He fought in the October 1862 Battle of Perryville, Kentucky, and the next spring trained as a mounted infantryman. In Tennessee in June, he fought at the Battle of Hoovers Gap, then in September took part in the Battle of Chickamauga in Georgia. There were running battles with Confederate cavalry in the weeks that followed Chickamauga. On October 7, Catlin's 123d Illinois skirmished with some Rebel horsemen at Farmington, Tennessee. When the two sides disengaged, thirteen Union men were left dead on the field. One of them was Stephen Catlin. The worst fears of his wife and daughters proved true.

Teenager George Catlin of the 5th Illinois Cavalry understood his duty to his family as well as to his country. In those times a boy was expected to provide for his widowed mother and sisters. When his enlistment expired in October 1864, he returned to Farmington to ensure the family's survival and to guarantee that the sacrifices of his father and brother were not forgotten

CHAPTER V
VETERANS

VETERANS

ALBERT WOOLSON OF MINNESOTA DIED IN 1956. Although he was a very old man, his passing was still remarkable enough that news of it won space in newspapers around the country and in national magazines. Woolson, once a drummer attached to a Union army artillery outfit, had been the country's last link with the Civil War military experience. He was America's last living Civil War soldier.

U.S. President Andrew Johnson declared an official end to hostilities at the end of 1865. At that point, a quick head count showed more than two million men claiming service in the Union or Confederate armed forces had survived the conflict, but survival was about all they had in common. What was in store for each added up to almost two million individual stories.

Gen. Robert E. Lee surrendered his Army of Northern Virginia at Appomattox, Virginia, on April 9. After dignified ceremonies in which the Rebels paraded one last time then stacked their arms and flags in front of saluting Union troops, Lee's enlisted men were allowed to make their own way home. There were similar scenes after Gen. Joseph E. Johnston surrendered his Army of the Tennessee to Gen. William Tecumseh Sherman in North Carolina on April 26, when Lt. Gen. Richard Taylor gave up his troops outside Mobile on May 4, and when Lt. Gen. E. Kirby Smith's men of the Trans-Mississippi military department were surrendered on May 26. On June 23, Brig. Gen. Stand Watie, a chief of the Cherokee and leader of a Southern force made up of Creek, Seminole, Cherokee, and Osage Indian

troops, rode into Doaksville, in what is now Oklahoma, and gave up his command. Stand Watie would go into the history books as the last Confederate general to surrender.

Through May and June, thousands of surrendered Confederate common soldiers went home, many going most of the way on foot, some traveling as far as from Virginia to Texas. Over those same weeks, Confederates were released from prisoner of war camps in places like upstate New York and Illinois after being asked to take an oath of allegiance to the United States.

There would be no U.S. government help of any kind for these men for the rest of their lives on any matter related to their Confederate service. They had attempted revolution and lost. In other places and in other times, there would be executions and reprisals against men such as these, rebels defeated by the government in power. Many understood this and were grateful for their lives and for the opportunity to start over. Others were bitter and would spend the rest of their days opposing Reconstruction and speaking reverently of "the Lost Cause." Still others refused to cope with the loss. Kirby Smith led three hundred men into Mexico to settle and start new lives. Over the next several months, thousands of Southern veterans followed. Still others moved farther away, one group of Rebel veterans establishing a colony in Brazil where their descendants live to this day.

Union troops had a different experience at the end of the Civil War. Demobilization was incredibly rapid. Throughout much of the country, after getting the official word that their nearest Confederate opponents had

Above: One of the last of his breed, an elderly Confederate veteran poses with his grandchild on Memorial Day. This photo was taken in the early 1920s. Opposite: Meeting the end of the war with relief, in July 1865 surviving members of the 4th Vermont Infantry muster out of service in the town of Brattleboro. The photograph was taken by G. W. Houghton, the same cameraman who earlier documented the unit's service in the field.

surrendered, regiments got a quick train ride back to the town where they were first organized. There the men stood for a brief mustering out ceremony, drew any outstanding pay due them, then wandered home, some going to work on family farms or into old jobs the very next day. Some elected to keep their service rifle for a fee of thirteen dollars. Those trophies hung over fireplaces in veterans' homes for decades.

Many of Grant's and Sherman's troops, located in the East, had a more lavish exit from the army. Washington, D.C., witnessed two consecutive days of parades. On May 23 Maj. Gen. George G. Meade led eighty thousand men of the Army of the Potomac down Pennsylvania Avenue past a reviewing stand occupied by President Johnson and dignitaries. Tens of thousands of spectators crowded the sidewalks to cheer. The scene was repeated the next day when Sherman led sixty-five thousand men of his Army of Georgia and Army of the Tennessee down the avenue and past the president. On both days, as each regiment completed its march, it was mustered out, and its men were paid and given train tickets home. That ended their service.

Downtown Selma, Alabama, in the 1870s, still waiting for some postwar prosperity.

No veteran, North or South, received any government medical assistance for old war wounds or service-connected illnesses. There was no such thing as psychiatric care for those traumatized by the war experience. For some, there was no work. Veterans crippled by wounds, left armless or legless by amputations, or blinded in the war begged on street corners or in barrooms and were the objects of charity. Individual northern and southern states established homes for disabled soldiers later in the century, many of them supported by fund drives, not tax dollars. In the months and years immediately after the war, the country was littered with maimed ex-soldiers. In that period, virtually no American was spared the sight of what war could do to a human mind or body.

Many other veterans found that their war experience gave them a leg up in life. In most of the North, for decades solid veteran credentials were expected of every man who held elected office. Following Reconstruction and the return of the vote to former Southern soldiers, a virtual company of "colonels" represented the states of Old Dixie in Congress. Travel during the war and exposure to people from around the country also filled the heads of some veterans with ideas. These men settled territories in the West, applied military engineering skills to civilian projects, invested in real estate or in railroad construction, contributed to the great spate of practical inventions that swarmed over the nation in the late nineteenth century, or made millions pursuing dreams they had put off during the war years.

In the postwar era when self-reliance was one of the paramount American virtues, the old Confederate and Union veterans showed themselves to be exceptionally so. They formed the Grand Army of the Republic and the United Confederate Veterans organizations to look after veteran interests in state government, to aid the widows and orphans of servicemen, and to promote community rebuilding and service. By the late 1800s each group had accomplished most of its missions. Members were then left with the benefit of the comradeship they grew to feel for other old soldiers. Perhaps it was what they enjoyed most about belonging to these outfits. In the twentieth century they held conventions, encampments, and reunions where they traded war stories. On some occasions, such as the 1913 gathering at Gettysburg on the fiftieth anniversary of the great battle, the old Yankees and Rebels came together and shook hands on spots where they had once fired at each other with deadly intent. News photos of these battlefield reconciliations never failed to make Americans feel better about the past or the future.

After World War I, the number of living Civil War veterans dropped dramatically. Their get-togethers became the objects of public curiosity. Probably none was more bittersweet than the 1951 convention of the United Confederate Veterans. All three of the organization's last living members attended. ✪

THOMAS C. HINDMAN

Once a fellow had held a rank and an opinion, it was sometimes hard for him to put either of them aside. On October 22, 1865—some months after the end of the Civil War—former Confederate Maj. Gen. Thomas C. Hindman put on his dress uniform one more time to sit for this photograph with his three children, reminding posterity and his family of what he had once been.

An unrepentant Secessionist from Arkansas, Hindman had difficulty bearing the defeat of his cause, and after this photograph was taken, he moved his family to Mexico to take up growing coffee. The Mexican venture quickly failed, and the petite ex-general (he stood just five feet one inch) went back to Arkansas to fight Reconstruction. There he fell victim to the rough-and-tumble politics of the times. He was assassinated in his Helena, Arkansas, home on September 28, 1868.

Not a very common man in his time, of the 425 individuals who held the rank of general in the Confederate army, the disabled Hindman (an eye wound in the 1864 Atlanta campaign put him out of service for the remainder of the war) is today one of the less well remembered.

THE CHILDREN OF GENERAL HOOD

Reminders of hard times for a distinguished veteran's children: These are the orphans of former Confederate Gen. John Bell Hood, a Southern soldier who lost the use of his left arm in the Battle of Gettysburg then lost his right leg in the Battle of Chickamauga. After Chickamauga, Hood was given command of the Army of Tennessee. He lost the city of Atlanta to General Sherman and the Battles of Franklin and Nashville to Union Gens. John M. Schofield and George H. Thomas.

Hood, a bachelor during the war, married in 1868, made his home in New Orleans, and worked as a commission merchant and in the insurance business. By 1879, when a yellow fever epidemic hit New Orleans, he was the father of eleven children—among them three sets of twins—and in poor financial shape. The general, his wife, and their eldest child died of the fever.

Former Confederate Gen. P. G. T. Beauregard and veterans of Hood's Texas Brigade arranged for the posthumous publication of Hood's war memoirs *Advance and Retreat*, hoping book sales would help support the children. Then they arranged for this photograph to be made. It was circulated nationally to help find adoptive homes for the orphans. The ten little Hoods were scattered to homes in both the North and South. In adulthood, only two of the ten married and produced children to carry on the general's family name.

JOHN A. WILSON

John A. Wilson enjoyed life in the decades that followed the Civil War. Not everyone was aware of that, though. Some thought he was dead. A native of Peoria, Wilson was a private in the 77th Illinois Volunteer Infantry when his unit assaulted Confederate defenses at Vicksburg, Mississippi, on May 22, 1863. As Wilson scaled the enemy earthworks, a Rebel shoved his rifle over the top and fired. The bullet penetrated the base of Wilson's nose, passed under his left eye, exited thorough his cheek, and lodged in his left shoulder. The impact sent him rolling in the ditch below where he laid unconcious with the dead and other wounded for hours.

When fighting stopped on that part of the line, an Illinois chaplain passed by, picking over bodies, looking for men from home. Rolling the unconcious Wilson over, he saw his nasty head wound and assumed the worst. The chaplain reported Wilson dead in a letter published by Peoria newspapers.

After dark Wilson regained consciousness and with help from another wounded man made his way to a field hospital. His brother, Samuel Wilson, also served in this theater of the war and eventually caught up with John convalescing in Memphis. He stayed with him for weeks, nursing him, then was transferred to the Mobile, Alabama, area. Samuel Wilson was killed in combat there in April 1865. John meanwhile recovered sufficiently to enter the Veteran Reserve Corps. Without returning to Peoria, he served in the reserve corps until 1867 then married and moved to Lynchburg, Virginia. He was an attorney and postmaster in Lynchburg, later served as mayor of Buchanan, Virginia, then retired to Lynchburg, where he passed away of natural causes in 1901 at age sixty-five. He died not knowing that for some time people passing through the national cemetery at Vicksburg saw a headstone with his name on it and that in Peoria a local war memorial listed his name and a death date for him: May 22, 1863.

MILTON A. BLICKENSDERFER

Milton A. Blickensderfer was a very ordinary man from Jefferson County, Ohio, and a veteran with a different story to tell. Married and a father of three children, he was twenty-seven years old and a sometime butcher and wagon maker when he enlisted in Company E, 126th Ohio in August 1862. He performed unexciting duties until his regiment was sent to New York City to put down draft riots in July 1863. After that he soldiered through the Wilderness, Spotsylvania, and Cold Harbor fights, and the Battle of Monocacy, Maryland. He was present for most of the siege of Petersburg, and for a while even held the rank of sergeant. Then Blickensderfer played a practical joke that his superiors didn't think was funny. He let out a Rebel yell in the middle of the night in his regiment's camp and panicked the other men. This got him busted back to corporal.

Before dawn on April 2, 1865, Blickensderfer joined in the final Union assault on Petersburg's defenses. His regiment stormed the earthworks south of the city. In the course of the fighting the corporal captured a Confederate battle flag. Throughout the Civil War this was considered one of the most courageous things a soldier could accomplish. The loss of a battle flag sent enemy units into retreat or disorganization; sometimes it compelled an entire army to fall back. Whole units had been known to be almost destroyed trying to capture a flag. The corporal's division managed to capture two other battle flags that day as the Southern defenses collapsed and Lee's army began its retreat. Yet Blickensderfer, the failed practical joker, managed to capture a battle flag on his own.

A month later Milton A. Blickensderfer was presented with the Medal of Honor—then and now his country's highest award for military valor. He went home, took up butchering and wagon making again, fathered six more children, and was able to die in peace at age eighty-one in Dover, Ohio, having known what it was to be both a very ordinary man and, in the official record, a very brave one.

WILLIAM H. SIMMS

Late in the nineteenth century, William H. Simms could look back on some bad luck during the Civil War and think of it instead as a profitable time investment. Born in Britain in 1845, Simms immigrated to Michigan with his family as a child and suffered poverty. An undernourished, undersized fellow in his late teens who supported his widowed mother and younger sister by working as a factory hand, he enlisted in Company L, 1st Michigan Engineers and Mechanics Regiment on December 17, 1863. The regiment built forts, bridges, and other military works, often under combat conditions. In December 1864 it was blasted off a train by an artillery assault near Christiana, Tennessee, and Simms was later captured and served time in prisoner of war camps in Georgia and Florida until the war ended.

The Michigan mechanic was finally released on April 29, 1865. During his incarceration his army pay had accumulated. Upon his return home, this pay was given to him in a lump sum along with mustering-out money. Back in Michigan, he took the cash and invested in local businesses. Decades of fortunate sales and reinvestments followed. By 1892, the one-time poor boy was wealthy, with holdings in California, Wyoming, and Illinois. He made his home in Gibson City, Illinois, served as commander of his local Grand Army of the Republic post, and looked back on his prison experience as the thing that helped him turn the financial corner.

WILLIAM HENRY CHAPMAN

This man's wartime experience gave him the job skills he would need in his peacetime occupation. This is Lt. Col. William Henry Chapman, photographed when he was a captain of Confederate artillery. A former University of Virginia undergraduate, Chapman first enlisted in a state artillery unit in 1861, but in spring 1863 he joined the 43d Battalion, Virginia Cavalry, which was led by Col. John S. Mosby. Mosby was the Rebel partisan and guerrilla leader who specialized in harassment of Union rear-echelon troops and in hit-and-run raids, showing up out of nowhere, hitting an objective, and disappearing again.

Mosby's phantom-like talents earned him the nickname "the Gray Ghost." Chapman studied his ways and became a close associate. When peace came, Mosby, an attorney in civilian life, put the past behind him and formed a personal and political bond with U.S. President Ulysses S. Grant. This brought him some patronage appointments, and he passed one on to Chapman. Mosby's former lieutenant colonel of raiders and guerrillas first worked for the railway mail service then found his niche as a Federal Revenue Service agent—a "revenuer"—hunting down moonshiners instead of Yankees.

Smashing stills and going after fellows who made illegal whiskey in the hills and backwoods of Virginia could be dangerous work. Chapman, though, must have been good at it. He died in retirement on September 13, 1929, in the middle of the Prohibition era, at age eighty-nine.

ALEXANDER BAILLIE KELL

This is a photograph of Alexander Baillie Kell during his brief stint as a second lieutenant in a local provisional military outfit, the McIntosh Company of Cavalry, organized near Darien, Georgia, in early 1861. For Kell—from landed Georgia gentry, educated at Princeton University and the Kentucky Military Institute, the brother of famous Confederate naval officer John McIntosh Kell, and described in records as "a high-toned gentleman"—this would be as good as things got for the remainder of his days, and those days would be many.

Kell, who managed the family estate and looked after the support of his widowed mother and two unmarried sisters, hesitated to pursue some military career options when his six months with the McIntosh Company ended. On May 19, 1862, he finally enlisted as a private in Company H, 5th Georgia Cavalry and hoped his background, education, and talents would win him advancement. This never occurred, however, despite letters of endorsement from his commanding officer and Gen. P. G. T. Beauregard to the Confederate War Department recommending him for an officer's commission. He served through the war as a private in a unit attached to Maj. Gen. Joseph Wheeler's cavalry opposing General Sherman's campaigns through Georgia. In spring 1865 he was surrendered along with the rest of the Army of Tennessee and paroled May 3.

Kell's family plantation, Laurel Grove, was in poor shape at war's end, and his mother and dependent sisters were still with him. He tried farming himself and rented Laurel Grove land to freed slaves. This brought little money. He worked as a civil engineer for the Rome and Carrolton Railroad, but the job didn't work out. When he was more than forty years old, his fiancée dumped him because she saw no promise in him. His family began to worry about his "lonely condition and unsettled frame of mind." His mother passed away, and his struggle to survive continued. In 1899, at age seventy-one, Kell applied for a state pension for indigent Confederate veterans, claiming paralyzed feet and rheumatism prevented him from working and that he was totally without means of support. In the end, he went to live with his brother John, then the state adjutant general, and remained with John's family until he died September 30, 1912.

MAHLON SPRAGUE

....

This veteran gave up his health in Union service and, living in a time when being able-bodied meant the difference between employment or poverty, ended up missing out on most of life's comforts for more than fifty years.

Mahlon Sprague was the twenty-three-year-old son of a sea captain with a farm at Trenton when he enlisted in Company E, 5th New Jersey Volunteers on August 19, 1861. Over the next four years he soldiered through the Peninsula campaign, the Second Battle of Bull Run, Chancellorsville, Gettysburg, the Wilderness, the October 1864 Battle of Poplar Springs Church, and the April 1865 Battle of Farmville, Virginia. At Chancellorsville he was wounded in the left arm by a shell fragment; in the Wilderness he was shot through the left foot; at Poplar Springs Church he was hit near a kneecap by a Confederate bullet that was almost—but not quite—spent.

Sprague mustered out of the army July 17, 1865, and went back to the Trenton farm. Work there was difficult, and eventually the crippling effects of his old war wounds forced him to give up manual labor. He spent the last years of his life in the New Jersey Home for Disabled Soldiers in Kearny. He died there February 6, 1921, at age eighty-three.

WILLIAM ASHLINE

This is a wartime photograph of William Ashline of Iowa. On August 15, 1862, together with his younger brother George and his older brothers Hiram and Edward, William enlisted in Company E, 27th Iowa Volunteer Infantry. The brothers' far-ranging adventures would make for interesting tales in the years to come.

With the 27th, William would serve until the end of the Civil War, campaigning after Confederate cavalry commander Nathan Bedford Forrest, taking part in the capture of Little Rock, Arkansas, fighting in the Red River campaign and the Battle of Pleasant Hill, Louisiana, the Battle of Nashville, and in the late-war campaign to take Mobile. One by one, however, the other Ashline brothers dropped out of the service. Edward was discharged from the army after the January 1863 chase pursuit of Forrest; he had contracted tuberculosis and would be dead of the disease within a year. In July 1863 George Ashline was shot in the right knee by a careless soldier from another company. Surgeons could not remove the bullet from the knee cartilage and sent him home for good in November of that year. Hiram trooped on through to the Confederate surrender, but as the 27th took up occupation duty he was sent home in June 1865 with an undisclosed disability.

After Hiram went home, William Ashline saw a little more service around Mobile then was transferred to Vicksburg, Mississippi, before being mustered out in Clinton, Iowa, on August 8, 1865. He died in Edgewood, Iowa, in 1919. Younger brother George would outlast him, living until 1927 and carrying that Union bullet in his knee until the day he died.

JOHN CHARLES RIETTI

At the outset of the Civil War, nineteen-year-old John Charles "Jack" Rietti of Jackson, Mississippi, signed up as a private with Company D, 10th Mississippi Infantry—the Mississippi Rifles—and posed for this photograph in the unit's custom uniform, a dark green coat and trousers with red trim and a Hungarian-style military hat. An enthusiastic soldier as well as a journeyman printer and journalist, Jack wrote a company song, "The Mississippi Rifles' Hymn, 1861."

Jack Rietti didn't take Southern military defeat very well. After rising to sergeant and serving in most of the war's brutal western campaigns, he was one of only sixty-four original members of the 10th Mississippi to make it home after being paroled with Lt. Gen. Stephen D. Lee's corps in May 1865. He closed his wartime diary with the words "Farewell Southern confederacy" then set about fighting the U.S. government's Reconstruction policies. In the town of Vicksburg in 1873, with partners John Cashman and Charlie Miller, he started publishing the *Daily Vicksburger*, a newspaper aimed at "the overthrow of the Radical Rule" that then afflicted the state, according to the publishers. The next year, with carpetbaggers and scalawags defeated in the election, Rietti and his associates were satisfied they had made their political points and ceased publication of their paper.

Rietti moved back to Jackson, worked there as a printer, and started research for what he hoped would be a series of books called *The Military Annals of Mississippi*, works dedicated to "That Host of Heroes of the Lost Cause." He published only one volume before his death on August 30, 1896, at age fifty-five.

ADOLPHUS WILLIAMSON MAGNUM

The Mangums were a distinguished North Carolina family. Several of them served the Confederacy during the Civil War. This family member, Adolphus Williamson Mangum, was briefly chaplain of the 6th North Carolina Infantry.

Adolphus Mangum's Civil War contribution is really one to history in general and to life in North Carolina in the days that followed the conflict. A Methodist pastor with a doctor of divinity degree, illness forced him to leave the army after several months' service. Back in North Carolina, for a time he served as chaplain to Union prisoners of war held at Salisbury Prison, where health and sanitation problems killed astounding numbers. By war's end, eleven thousand bodies had been buried in trenches outside the prison's confines. Only about one-third of the dead were identified. The reason

any were known, however, was because their deaths occurred during A. W. Mangum's tenure as chaplain. He officiated at every burial and recorded all details. Others who came after him apparently did not do these things. In postwar years this information helped relieve the distress of some families and later proved useful to historians.

Mangum's greatest contribution to society occurred later when he helped reopen the University of North Carolina at Chapel Hill, an institution closed and debilitated by the war. Initially one of only twelve faculty members, he ended up teaching law, science, literature, and religion. As the institution grew so did his esteem within it. Today, Mangum Dormitory there is named to honor him and other family members who supported the school. Mangum died in Chapel Hill in 1890 at age fifty-six.

WILLARD WHEELER NYE

This is Willard Wheeler Nye. At the time this photograph was taken, he was a very slightly built, underweight fourteen-year-old. How he talked his way into enlistment is not known, but the 23d Illinois Regiment took him as their drummer boy.

With the 23d, Nye was besieged and captured at Lexington, Missouri, in 1861. Later released, Nye then enlisted with his friend Capt. Edgar Trego in the 8th Kansas Infantry. With Trego as his protector, he served in Kentucky and Georgia. Then during the September 1863 Battle of Chickamauga, Trego was killed. Nye served on through the fights for Chattanooga that November then fell ill in December. He was discharged for poor health, but once his strength returned, Nye enlisted again, this time in a short-term unit called the 139th Illinois. That proved to be his last hitch.

After discharge in October 1864, Willard Nye looked to his own development. He studied medicine and moved to Hiawatha, Kansas, where he served the town as physician until well into the twentieth century. Perhaps it was the poor army rations or the exertion or sleeping in the bad weather, but Nye never grew much after his army service. At his biggest he measured in at a height of five feet. When he died in Hiawatha in 1938 at age ninety-two, he was still called "the little doctor."

THE UNKNOWN VETERAN

Into the twentieth century, Union and Confederate veterans made sure the public remembered what they did in the 1860s. As members of organizations such as the Grand Army of the Republic and the United Confederate Veterans, they lobbied state legislatures and the U.S. Congress for bills favoring their interests, established the Memorial Day holiday, and erected plaques, statues, and monuments on old battlefield sites.

This nameless Confederate veteran was one of approximately twelve thousand who descended on Little Rock, Arkansas, in May 1911 for the last, large United Confederate Veterans reunion and a display of emotional muscle.

In front of a crowd estimated at 150,000, these elderly men paraded for twenty blocks, accompanied by fourteen marching bands. This old Southern army drummer collapsed in the heat, but on being revived he posed for this portrait, standing straight and tall. On the occasion of the fiftieth anniversary of the start of the Civil War, he was one of the few left to represent the approximate one million men who had served in the Confederate armed forces.

He and others like him North and South were determined not to fade away. As long as one common soldier of the Civil War breathed, he would speak for the others and for what they had done, endured, and sacrificed.

PICTURE CREDITS

Page 3: print from *Civil War Times Illustrated* collection. **4:** Burton Historical Collection, Detroit Public Library. **6:** Washington, D.C. volunteers, Rhode Island Historical Society **8:** NA. **9:** LC. **10:** NA. **12:** Kentucky Historical Society, Kentucky Military History Museum, Frankfort, KY. **13:** USAMHI. **14, left:** USAMHI. **14, right:** print from *Civil War Times Illustrated* collection. **15, left:** Chicago Historical Society. **15, center, top:** Herb Peck Jr. collection. **15, center, bottom:** NA. **15, right:** Courtesy of Baltimore and Ohio Railroad Museum, Inc. **16, left:** NA. **16, right:** Courtesy of Mrs. Albert McBride. **17:** Courtesy, Arkansas History Commission. **18–19:** print from *Civil War Times Illustrated* collection. **21:** U.S. Air Force. **22:** New-York Historical Society. **23, left:** Print and Picture Collection, Free Library of Philadelphia. **23, right:** LC. **24:** Lloyd Ostendorf Collection, Dayton, OH. **25, top:** USAMHI. **25, bottom:** LC. **26, left:** Herb Peck Jr. Collection. **26, right:** LC. **27:** USAMHI. **28:** Vermont Historical Society. **29:** Vermont Historical Society. **31:** NA. **32–33:** print from *Civil War Times Illustrated* collection. **35:** USAMHI. **36:** Joe M. Bauman. **37:** print from *Civil War Times Illustrated* collection. **38:** Courtesy of the Burton Historical Collection, Detroit Public Library. **39:** Alabama Department of Archives and History, Montgomery, AL. **40:** Herb Peck Jr. Collection. **41:** USAMHI. **42:** Valentine Museum, Richmond, VA. **43:** Lloyd Ostendorf Collection, Dayton, OH. **45:** Tim Landis, New York, NY. **46:** Lloyd Ostendorf Collection, Dayton, OH. **47, left:** William O. Walcott, South Laguna, CA. **47, center:** Jack G. Grothe. **47, right:** Edward J. Lenc, Parma, OH. **48:** Tennessee State Library and Archives. **49:** Tennessee State Museum. **51:** Chesley C. Herndon Jr., Oklahoma City, OK. **52, all:** Alabama Department of Archives and History, Montgomery, AL. **53, left:** E. Marita Fields, Marion, IN. **53, right:** Robert H. Moore II, Havelock, NC. **54, left:** Herb Peck Jr. Collection. **54, center:** John T. Spach. **54, right:** print from *Civil War Times Illustrated* collection. **55:** Thomas Atwood, Vernon Hills, IL. **57:** H. David Williams and John Cottier, Valdosta State College. **58:** Mike Fitzpatrick, Rockville, MD. **59, left:** William A. Tidwell, Hyattsville, MD. **59, right:** Clark B. Hall, Carrollton, GA. **60:** William Dodd Brown, Chicago, IL. **61:** Ohio Historical Society. **62:** David A. Patience, Salem, OR. **63:** Dale S. Snair, Atlanta, GA. **64–65:** Florida State Archives. **66–67:** Les Jensen Collection. **69:** USAMHI. **70:** Kean Wilcox Collection. **71:** Lloyd Ostendorf Collection, Dayton, OH. **72:** The Museum of

the Confederacy, Richmond, VA. **73:** Herb Peck Jr. Collection. **74:** USAMHI. **75, right:** USAMHI. **75, center:** USAMHI. **75, right:** Michael J. McAfee. **76–77:** NA. **78, top:** Collection of Old Capitol Museum of Mississippi History, Jackson, MS. **78, bottom left:** print from *Civil War Times Illustrated* collection. **78, bottom right:** USAMHI. **79:** Stan Cosby, Tulsa, OK. **80, top:** Barbara Overton Christie, Westbrook, CT. **80, bottom left:** NA. **80, bottom right:** USAMHI. **81:** Wendell Lang, Tarrytown, NY. **82:** Barry I. Mickey, Cleveland, MS. **83:** USAMHI. **84:** Garry Bryant, Salt Lake City, UT. **85:** USAMHI. **86:** Allan W. Heath, Jonesboro, GA. **87:** both USAMHI. **88:** Albert E. Hunter, Bozman, MD. **89, left:** Lawrence J. German, Cleveland, TN. **89, right:** John B. Bailey, Douglasville, GA. **90:** Dean Knudson, Colfax, IO. **91, top:** Minnesota Historical Society. **91,**

Bergstresser's Photographic Studio,
3rd Division, 5th Corps, Army of the Potomac.

bottom: USAMHI. **92:** Panhandle-Plains Historical Museum Research Center, Canyon, TX. **93:** Ursaline Academy Library. **94, left:** Blake Smith, Gatesville, TX. **94, right:** Ed Hill, Cartersville, GA. **95:** Alexander P. Petrie, Atwood, IL. **96:** Bill McFarland, Topeka, KS. **97:** USAMHI. **98:** W. J. Kierstead, Union, NJ. **99, both:** Chicago Historical Society. **100, all:** Alabama Department of Archives and History, Montgomery, AL. **101:** Rayford L. Cannon, Saylacauga, AL, and Edwin W. Besch, Mobile, AL. **102–3:** print from *Civil War Times Illustrated* collection. **104:** USAMHI. **105:** USAMHI. **106:** Rhinehart Galleries, Inc. **107:** John W. Brinsfield. **108, left:** from a copy at Jones Memorial Library, Lynchburg, VA. **108, center:** Horace Mathews. **108, right:** USAMHI. **109, left:** Spencer H. Waterson, Pontiac, IL. **109, right:** courtesy State Archives of Michigan. **110:** Gordon A. Cotton, Vicksburg, MS. **111:** Robert G. Carroon, West Hartfort, CT. **112, both:** William Gladstone, Westport, CT. **113, left:** USAMHI. **113,**

right: NA. **114, left:** John M. Archer, Collinsville, CT. **114, right:** Martin J. Urner, Hagerstown, MD. **115, left:** Darlington County Historical Society, SC. **115, right:** Carpenter King, Darlington, SC. **116, top:** NA. **116, bottom:** Wendell Lang, Tarrytown, NY. **117, left:** Carl F. Heinz III, Lancaster, CA. **117, right:** St. Lawrence University Libraries. **118:** Marian B. Ralph. **119:** Barnaby Conrad, Carpinteria, CA. **120:** James M. Templeton Jr., Gonzales, LA. **121:** Gregory J. Urwin, Conway, AR. **122:** Dr. Royce G. Shingleton, Albany, GA. **123:** LC. **124, left, right:** Thomas E. Bowen Jr. and Steven Burgess, Romoland, CA. **124, center:** Chicago Historical Society. **125:** Gregory J. Johnson, State College, PA. **126, left, right:** Minnesota Historical Society. **126, center:** Louisville and Nashville Railroad Historical Society. **127:** Heidi and Holly Hewitt, Crossville, TN. **128–29:** William Gladstone, Eastport, CT. **130:** USAMHI. **131:** USAMHI. **132:** NA. **133:** LC. **134:** Fanny U. Phillips. **135, top:** Valentine Museum, Richmond, VA. **135, bottom:** LC. **136, all:** USAMHI. **137:** Curt Schmidt, Medina, OH. **138, both:** Michael D. Jones, Iowa, LA. **139:** Richard K. Tibbals, Oak Park, IL. **140, both:** Kirk R. Sellman, Tigard, OR. **141, both:** LC. **142, 143:** Frank M. Bushnell. **144:** Richard F. Carlile, Dayton, OH. **145, left:** Richard F. Carlile, Dayton, OH. **145, right:** Terry N. McGinnis, Kansas City, MO. **146:** Michael J. McAfee. **149:** William Gladstone, Eastport, CT. **150:** Richard H. Moy, Springfield, IL. **151:** USAMHI. **152, left:** New Market Battlefield Park, New Market, VA. **152, right:** USAMHI. **153:** Neill W. Macaulay, Columbia, SC. **154, both:** USAMHI. **155:** William F. Howard, Delmar, NY. **156:** USAMHI. **157:** Glenn Dedmondt, Tryon, NC. **158:** Mark R. Brewer, Mount Laurel, NJ. **159:** LC. **161:** LC. **161:** Richard Milhollin Coffman, Columbia, SC. **162, top:** Ronn Palm collection. **162, bottom:** USAMHI. **163:** Charles E. Pearson, Baton Rouge, LA. **164:** Mark Dunkelman and Mike Winey. **165:** LC. **167:** Richard W. Ruhanen Jr., Toivola, MN. **168–69:** Ray Hanley, Little Rock, AR. **170:** print from *Civil War Times Illustrated* collection. **171:** Vermont Historical Society. **172:** print from *Civil War Times Illustrated* collection. **173:** Bob Younger Collection. **174:** Confederate Museum, New Orleans, LA. **175:** Conrad Eckert, Tulsa, OK. **176:** Kenneth D. Fryer, Chester, VA. **178:** Dr. Thomas P. Lowry, Ross, CA. **179:** Robert H. Moore II, Havelock, NC. **181:** Dr. Norman C. Delaney, Corpus Christi, TX. **182:** Melvin Schurter, Cream Ridge, NJ. **183:** Allan W. Heath, Jonesboro, GA. **185:** H. Donaldson Thorp, Delray Beach, FL. **186:** Alan Whitehead, Greenwood, MS. **187:** William Preston Mangum II, Chapel Hill, NC. **188:** Kathleen B. Thiriot, Metairie, LA. **191:** Ray Hanley, Little Rock, AR. **192:** USAMHI.